# Creative Thinking in PHOTOSHOP®

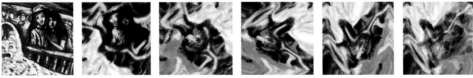

## A NEW APPROACH TO DIGITAL ART

### SHARON STEUER

201 West 103rd Street, Indianapolis, Indiana 46290
An Imprint of Pearson Education
Boston ▪ Indianapolis ▪ London ▪ New York ▪ San Francisco

# Creative Thinking in Photoshop

Copyright © 2002 by Sharon Steuer

International Standard Book Number: 0-7357-1122-4

Library of Congress Catalog Card Number: 20-01086185

Printed in the United States of America

First Printing: April 2002

06   05   04   03   02          7   6   5   4   3   2   1

Interpretation of the printing code: The rightmost double-digit number is the year of the book's printing; the rightmost single-digit number is the number of the book's printing. For example, the printing code 02-1 shows that the first printing of the book occurred in 2002.

## Trademarks

## Warning and Disclaimer

**Publisher**
David Dwyer

**Associate Publisher**
Stephanie Wall

**Production Manager**
Gina Kanouse

**Managing Editor**
Kristy Knoop

**Acquisitions Editor**
Linda Anne Bump

**Development Editor**
John Rahm

**Project Editor**
Suzanne Pettypiece

**Copy Editor**
Chrissy Andry

**Product Marketing Manager**
Kathy Malmloff

**Publicity Manager**
Susan Nixon

**Manufacturing Coordinator**
Jim Conway

**Cover Designer**
Aren Howell

**Interior Designer**
Kim Scott

**Compositor**
Kim Scott

**Proofreader**
Jeannie Smith

**Indexer**
Lisa Stumpf

# Contents at a Glance

# Table of Contents

## About the Author

**Sharon Steuer** is a painter and illustrator who works in traditional and digital media. An artist in traditional media beginning with crayons, since 1983 she has been a pioneer in the development of the computer as a fine-art medium; Photoshop has been her primary digital tool for over a decade. Steuer's computer paintings have appeared in numerous books and magazines, and she has taught computer imaging in art schools and training centers throughout the United States. She is a recipient of the national Faber Birren Color Award and is the author of *The Illustrator Wow! Book* series, which twice received the Benjamin Franklin Award as "the best computer book." Steuer can be reached at **studio@ssteuer.com**.

## About the Technical Editors

**Lisa Jackmore** is a freelance graphic artist living in northern Virginia. She has contributed her work to several editions of *The Illustrator Wow! Book*. As a native New Yorker, all of her learning was completed in Rhode Island—the hard stuff at Providence College and the fun stuff at The Rhode Island School of Design. Although Adobe Photoshop and Illustrator are her main tools, she also creates silly clay sculptures often inspired by the adventures of her son, Sam.

**Sandra Alves** currently works for Adobe Systems, Inc. as the lead user interface designer for Photoshop. Prior to this, Sandra had a 14-year career as a scientific/medical illustrator at UCSD, School of Medicine and Scripps Research Institute. In addition to her full-time career, she teaches, is co-author of *The Illustrator 9 Wow! Book*, is a mother of two awesome daughters, and likes to snowboard and water ski with her husband.

# Dedication

*To Bernie Chaet and all my wonderful art teachers without whom I wouldn't have the tools to express myself. To Archie Rand for daring me to express myself in more than just pretty pictures, and to Luciana for helping me to focus on what's important. And to my wonderful family and beloved friends, who always believed in me, and without whom nothing else would matter.*

## Acknowledgments

The first thank you must go to Bert Monroy for being truly inspirational in the development of the computer as an art medium, for recommending me to New Riders, and for being a kind and inclusive friend since the days when you could count the pixels across the screen. Thank you also Steve Weiss, Linda Bump, and John Rahm at New Riders for making this book happen and for being so patient in the first stages of the process. Thanks also must go to the many folks at New Riders who took raw text and pictures and made them into this book: Kim Scott for creating the spectacular art-book design for this book, Aren Howell for the elegant cover design, Suzanne Pettypiece for overseeing the entire project so fabulously, Chrissy Andry for the copy editing, Jeannie Smith for the proofreading and Lisa Stumpf for the index. And of course thank you Susan Nixon, Linda Buehler, and the marketing team for helping to get the word out about this book. Thanks to photographer Robert Lisak for my new head shot, and to Alani Gandossy for the digital photos in the intro. Thanks to Elizabeth Rogalin who is sometimes better at finding my words than I am. And thanks to Lisa Jackmore and Sandy Alves for taking the time to make sure the projects worked smoothly as planned.

Thank you Norma Holt for being my upstairs mother, for our wonderful collaborative time, and for giving me permission to include your work in this book. Thanks also to Jill Sablosky and Glen Gate for giving me permission to include the simulations of installations that I created for them. And thank you mom, Jeff, and all my clients who allowed me to include their likenesses, snapshots, and commissions in this book.

Special thanks to Adobe for including me in the Photoshop process, to Wacom for the wonderful Intuos tablets, and to Epson for allowing me to use the fabulous Epson 2000P printer to proof my images as well as to create fine art digital prints. Thank you to Peter and Sandy Koons at irisprints.com for the beautiful high-resolution scans and for producing my fine art digital reproductions.

Thanks also to Barbara Hawkins for believing in me and hiring me for those first teaching gigs and to Katrin Eismann for bailing me out of that first Photoshop teaching gig. And thanks to Ted Nace and Linnea Dayton for giving me the opportunity to produce my first book, *The Illustrator Wow! Book.*

Of course thanks to Sandee Cohen for our alternating exchanges of ranting, brainstorming, and identities. Thank you to my sister, Samantha, for encouraging me to find a healthy life-balance, to my brother, Arthur, for being so giving and loving, and to my new sister, Ariadne, for opening her heart to her new family. Thank you mom, Howie, Doris, and Frank for your constant love and support. Thanks to all those friends who by power of your caring and encouragement have become my family as well. And thank you, Jeff, for coming-up with the title of this book, and more importantly, for being my true love.

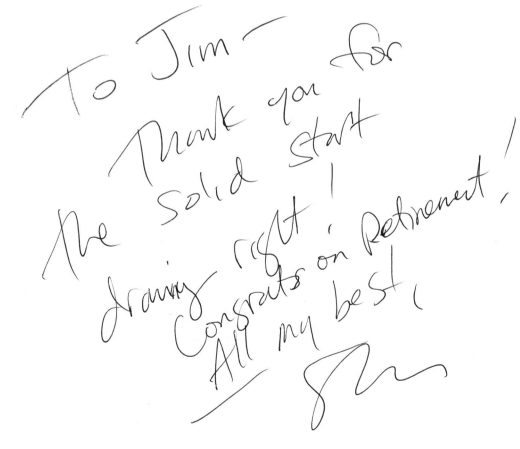

## A Message from New Riders

As the reader of this book, you are our most important critic and commentator. We value your opinion and want to know what we're doing right, what we could do better, in what areas you'd like to see us publish, and any other words of wisdom you're willing to pass our way.

As the Associate Publisher at New Riders, I welcome your comments. You can fax, email, or write me directly to let me know what you did or didn't like about this book—as well as what we can do to make our books better. When you write, please be sure to include this book's title, ISBN, and author, as well as your name and phone or fax number. I will carefully review your comments and share them with the authors and editors who worked on the book.

*Please note that I cannot help you with technical problems related to the topic of this book, and that due to the high volume of email I receive, I might not be able to reply to every message. Thanks.*

Fax:      317-581-4663

Email:    stephanie.wall@newriders.com

Mail:     Stephanie Wall
          Associate Publisher
          New Riders Publishing
          201 West 103rd Street
          Indianapolis, IN 46290 USA

### Visit Our Web Site: www.newriders.com

On our web site, you'll find information about our other books, the authors we partner with, book updates and file downloads, promotions, discussion boards for online interaction with other users and with technology experts, and a calendar of trade shows and other professional events with which we'll be involved. We hope to see you around.

### Email Us from Our Web Site

Go to **www.newriders.com** and click on the Contact Us link if you

- Have comments or questions about this book.

- Want to report errors that you have found in this book.

- Have a book proposal or are interested in writing for New Riders.

- Would like us to send you one of our author kits.

- Are an expert in a computer topic or technology and are interested in being a reviewer or technical editor.

- Want to find a distributor for our titles in your area.

- Are an educator/instructor who wants to preview New Riders books for classroom use. In the body/comments area, include your name, school, department, address, phone number, office days/hours, text currently in use, and enrollment in your department, along with your request for either desk/examination copies or additional information.

# Foreword

Back in the early days of computer graphics (before there were classes or books), we didn't worry about what we didn't know—we just made art and learned how the programs worked along the way. As programs grew, we gradually learned more, which is still the way we work. When I'm presenting at a conference, people inevitably ask me how I learned to do this or that, and most often the answer is "by experimenting!" Sharon encourages you to learn Photoshop the way we did—while you're making art and being creative.

I first met Sharon back in the early days of the digital revolution. She was furiously working away, doing portraits of attendees at a computer trade show. She gave each person a printout of his or her portrait as a memento, which was very effective in drawing a crowd to the booth. She was very good at it, and I managed to get myself immortalized by her handy work as well. The printout was an old dot-matrix printer output.

Sharon was at the next show I attended, sitting in someone else's booth—painting away. Her work really made the computer seem like an artist's tool at a time when there was much debate about whether computer art was in fact art. It is people like Sharon that provide evidence that the computer is simply a medium by which artists create their art. Sharon, in my opinion, is truly an artist extraordinaire. Her work can be whimsical and playful. At other times it can be dramatic and stirring. But whatever her direction or intent, it definitely draws the viewer into a moment of reflection. This book is a wonderful exploration into the mind of Sharon Steuer. You follow her progression through the creation process, giving you an insight into what motivates and drives her.

A perfectionist, she always wants things to be "just right." Well guess what—she did it. Here is a book that will be helpful and inspirational to anyone embarking on a journey of digital exploration. Whether you are a novice or an accomplished artist, you will enjoy traveling through Sharon's work process. Whether she is describing how to work with Layer Masks or explaining the concept of nonlinear creativity, she does it with a flair that is uniquely Sharon—entertaining and educational.

Sharon is a pleasure to know and now you too can get to know what makes her tick.

**—Bert Monroy**

# Introduction

Whether you're new to digital tools or are a seasoned veteran, whether you're dissatisfied with the work you're doing or are confident and creative with Photoshop, the goal of this book is to help you find new ways to integrate digital tools into your creative process.

Because the focus of this book is creativity, I've limited the amount of technical information covered in each project. If you're already a wizard with Photoshop, you should be able to sail through much of the technical instruction and focus immediately on the essence of creative suggestions. If you're a beginning Photoshop user, you'll likely move more slowly through the technical details. The amount of technical detail is more concentrated in the earlier chapters and decreases in a measured way as the book moves forward. If a project inspires you to gain more technical expertise in a particular area of Photoshop, see the books and authors that I recommend at the end of the "Arranging Your Workspace" appendix. Be patient with yourself. Remember that the goal of these projects is to help you focus on the creative *process*.

When I began to create artwork on the computer back in 1983, the technology was so basic that the few tools available were extremely simple. To create any image at all, I first had to figure out how each of the tools worked; in the process of experimenting with the tools, I would actually create artwork. Little by little, as the technology improved, more tools and functions became available, and I gradually integrated them into the way I work. My early digital artwork looked like it was created on the computer, but the technology was so basic that it didn't interfere with my creative process.

In 1992 by the time I had established Photoshop as my primary creative digital tool, I'd worked on more than a dozen different imaging programs—on more than six computer platforms. These imaging programs ranged from extremely simplistic to having significantly more functionality in some areas than the version of Photoshop I'm using at the time of this writing. But in all cases I experimented with the tools, learned what was unique about the program, and along the way created artwork.

Obviously the world of computer graphics is completely different now. Programs such as Photoshop or Illustrator are so complex that learning the tools and functions has actually become an obstacle to being creative.

Many artists and photographers are so overwhelmed by the myriad of digital tools in graphics programs today that they are too intimidated to work on the computer at all. Others take the time to explore the deep recesses of a program such as Photoshop but end up so seduced by the technology that they can't see beyond compositing or retouching scans and photos. Still other artists use the computer to merely mimic the way they work traditionally.

Photo by Alani Gandossy

But Photoshop is more than just a collection of cool tools. If you allow yourself to play and experiment creatively in Photoshop, you'll begin to think digitally. Thinking digitally will not only allow you to think creatively in Photoshop, but it also has the potential to enhance every aspect of your creative process.

Because programs and technology are constantly improving and changing and because the purpose of this book is to help you open up new ways of working using digital tools,

I've decided to include some works created in other programs. Whether you're working in Photoshop 4, 6, or 12, Quantel's Paintbox or Pro-Create's Painter, the concepts covered in this book should open your mind to new artistic possibilities, spark your imagination, and encourage you to develop your own ways of working creatively with the computer.

When people find out that I still work with traditional artists' materials as well as on the computer, they often ask me which I prefer. The media and methods are so different; each has its own place in my creative life.

Traditional painting for me is very physical. I usually paint standing. While holding brushes in my left hand, I paint with my right, sometimes using my whole arm. I stand back, move forward. I work in a space in which I am surrounded by past and current work. It is a very tactile, visual, sensory experience—and physical. I listen to loud music and dance around when I am painting. On the computer I sit with a tablet in my lap, holding the tablet stylus in one hand, the other on the keyboard. I listen to soft music or none at all and look up at a computer screen. When I feel like being more sedentary and quiet, I work on the computer. When I just have to be physical and move around, I paint. Sometimes I want to work neatly and controlled on the computer, while other times I need to work in mural-sized painted gestures. The two mediums are very different artistic impulses for me.

Despite the physical reality of creating computer images, I think of the computer as a printmaking tool. Digital output is generally flat and printed, whereas paintings are physically textural and tactile. Works on the computer also are similar to traditional printmaking in that there is often a degree of surprise when you see the printed piece. No matter how experienced artists feel themselves to be, there's often an element of, "Wow, that's not exactly what I had in mind," that comes with printmaking. This reaction is mostly a result of working in one medium, the printmaking plate or the computer, and displaying your final version of it in another medium, printed on paper. There also is the textural difference between a printmaking plate or a monitor screen and paper, as well as the added factor that computer monitors project light, whereas prints merely reflect light.

One advantage that traditional media has over computers is the specificity of "mark-making." If I am holding a pencil in my hand, I can achieve a subtlety and precision in drawing that I haven't yet been able to attain with a tablet and a computer. Whereas the computer provides artists with a bit less control in drawing, the computer makes up for this lack of precision in many other ways. The computer gives us an incredible amount of flexibility in terms of being able to edit marks. I might immediately "undo" (which I think was one of the great inventions of the 20th century), go over the mark continuously, or keep erasing without having to worry about destroying the integrity of the paper. On the computer there is no such thing as overworking anything—you can always undo or return to a previous saved state. Any saved stage can be later turned into a final state or can be reworked entirely.

The computer offers artists infinite opportunities to pursue what I call *nonlinear creativity*. Various states of work can be preserved and then can be reviewed and used later as springboards for further work. Any piece of art can be combined with others in various nonlinear ways to create endlessly exciting possibilities.

Working on the computer also makes me more daring creatively. I can take risks because I don't have to worry about losing anything. When I get to a point when I think, "Well this is good. I am not sure if it is done, but it's good," I can save it and then keep pushing on. Even at the point where I know the piece is done, I can still keep pushing. I can go beyond that sense of completion and explore what happens next. I can always undo or return to any previously saved state. Interestingly, I find working on the computer makes me more daring when I am in my painting studio. There are times when I'm painting in my studio when I suddenly realize, "Oh my God, I can't undo!" Ultimately, I view this as a good thing, that the computer is helping me to become more daring artistically in all media.

What excites me more than anything about working on the computer is that it has completely changed the way I work artistically, far beyond being more daring. Knowing I can combine multiple drawings to create a composited drawing allows me to work differently. If I am facing a stumbling block in a painting and don't know where to go compositionally (if it has been sitting in my studio for months or even years), I can scan that painting, bring it into the computer, and experiment with it freely. I can play with all sorts of ideas, print several out, bring them back into my studio, and go on. With photography you can shoot knowing that perhaps none of the photographs in the sequence you are taking is the perfect photograph, but that you can take an element from one and an element from another and make the piece that you were hoping to. Creatively, the computer allows you to do things you can't do any other way. By experimenting on the computer you can work through creative blocks and bring your work to a whole new level—both on the computer and off.

Throughout this book, I'll be using my artwork as examples of different approaches to integrating digital tools into the creative process. Different aspects of some of the projects will appear in various guises in various chapters. If I feel that a particular detail of a project will help illustrate a point, I'll include it. With luck, the imagery will be familiar and cohesive as you go, but if you're looking for other stages of a project that interests you, refer to "Techniques at a Glance" or the index for information.

Don't worry about memorizing or mastering, but instead concentrate on the concepts. Try not to focus on whether a specific project uses drawn or photographic imagery. It is not my hope that you replicate my process but use it as a jumping off point from which to explore and experiment with your own projects. Have fun with your work!

Photo by Alani Gandossy

CHAPTER 1

# Compositing and the Creative Process

As long as there has been Photoshop, artists and photographers have used it to combine their images. But to me, what's really exciting about compositing in Photoshop is how my entire creative process is affected by just knowing that I *can* combine images.

Although I implement aspects of the compositing process throughout this book, this chapter focuses on different ways I've integrated compositing techniques into my workflow. Try not to focus on whether a specific project involves drawings or photographs, is in black and white or color, or even includes techniques you've already mastered, but instead look at how integrating the concept of compositing at different phases in a project can impact the creative process. It's my hope that you'll not only discover new ways to expand your creative options with compositing, but maybe even radically change the way you create your source materials.

A composited photo combining seven 35mm shots taken with a 50mm lens.

A composited image incorporating four versions of scanned drawings.

## The Basics of the Compositing Process

Basic compositing is really a four-step process:

1. Digitizing your images (getting your images into Photoshop).

2. Placing the images you want to composite into one file.

3. Scaling the images so they fit properly together.

4. Controlling which portion of each image is visible.

Depending on the specifics of your project, the order of the last two steps is interchangeable.

How I get my images into Photoshop varies from project to project and ranges from digital photography to a variety of scanning technologies to painting directly into Photoshop. However you digitize your images, it's important to remember that although Photoshop is really good at throwing out information when it scales images down, it's pretty poor at guessing how to add extra pixels when you scale something up. Therefore, it's important to digitize your images at the maximum resolution that you might possibly need and always plan on scaling down—not up.

## Keeping the Old While Bringing in the New

Whether or not you intend to use digital tools from the outset, try to stay open to the idea of integrating the computer into any project that requires changes. Especially when you're working on a commercial project or you're on a tight deadline, it can be preferable to patch in an isolated change digitally—rather than have to reshoot or redraw the entire original. In the project that follows, instead of continually editing my original drawing, I ended up compositing elements in Photoshop that I created separately. The resulting final image wasn't the traditional drawing that I started out to create, but instead turned out to be a digital original made up of three separate incomplete drawings.

For this project I was commissioned to create a drawing of a client's house as viewed from a distance. The house sits on a point of land that juts onto the Long Island Sound. When I began the first drawing of "The Point," as my client calls it, I had no intention of using digital technology. As the project progressed and as the client requested more modifications to the drawing, I began to consider digitally compositing separate drawings and delivering a digital final image instead. After I'd made that decision, my approach to the project changed. I was able to preserve any aspect of any drawing I liked without having to redraw it. I created separate partial drawings as needed, which I composited in Photoshop to create a new, digital final image.

Working from a series of photographs of the property taken by the client, I first drew the long shot drawing in pencil and paper, assuming this drawing would be the final image (Figure 1.1). When I made the first corrections to the drawing, I of course used a traditional pencil and eraser.

In her initial feedback, the client requested that I render more specific detailing on the house. I realized that the scale of the original drawing was too tiny for me to include the requested amount of detail. Instead of redrawing the entire composition larger (and risk losing the qualities of the drawing the client and I liked), I decided to use the computer to composite this original drawing with any other details or corrections that I needed.

I next drew a separate drawing of the house in a scale big enough for me to incorporate more detail (Figure 1.2).

**1.1** The original drawing of "The Point."

**1.2** When you're ready to combine your elements, first decide which image will be your main image. (If there isn't a clear dominant image, then choose your lowest resolution or smallest scale image as the main image so you can scale other elements down to fit.)

When you do combine images that were shot or created at a different scale, one of the elements must be scaled to fit the other. Because the original long shot drawing and the detail drawing were approximately the same physical size, I planned to use Photoshop to scale the Detail image down to fit within the long shot. Because I knew that Photoshop is so good at reducing images, I scanned both the original and the detail drawings into the computer in grayscale, at 300 pixels per inch, and saved each as a separate TIFF file.

To move a source image into a main image, make sure that both images are open in Photoshop and visible at the same time. You can then use the Move tool to drag and drop the source image (or a current selection within the image) on top of the main image. Another way to bring in the image is to drag and drop the image's layer from the Layers palette to the main image (make sure you grab the layer containing the image). If you hold down the Shift key when you drop the source image into your main image, the source image will be centered within the main image (and properly registered if the files are the same size).

After both of my images were digitized, I dragged the Detail image into the long shot image. Next, I saved the long shot file, which now contained both images (each on its own layer) as a Photoshop format file called "Main Image."

Whether you've dragged and dropped from the image or the image's Layers palette, the new source image will be added to your main file—on its own layer. You should rename the layer meaningfully in Layer Properties. In some versions of Photoshop, you double-click a layer name to rename it; in others you'll have to hold the Option key for Mac or Alt key for Windows when you double-click. Make sure to save the new combined file with a new name and in Photoshop format to preserve the layer information.

After a source image is added to your main file, you'll often have to scale the image on that layer to fit within the main image. An easy way to do this is to target the layer you want to scale by clicking it in the Layers palette and then choosing the Free Transform command (Command+T for Mac or Ctrl+T for Windows).

While you can adjust the size of the active transformation from any handle, to scale down a layer proportionately, grab a corner handle and drag inward while holding the Shift key down. To access the Zoom-in tool while a transformation is in process, press Command+Spacebar (Mac) or Ctrl+Spacebar (Windows) and add the Option key (Mac) or Alt key (Windows) to access the Zoom-out tool.

Because I usually scale from a corner, I often have to nudge the selection back into position to fine-tune the scaling. The first way to nudge an active transformation is to move your cursor inside the transformation area until it turns into an arrow and then drag the transformation to its new location. Alternatively, you can use the left, right, up, and down cursor key arrows on the keyboard. When you're absolutely sure that a transformation is correct, note the scaling percentage in the info bar (in case you need it again). Remember, you want to avoid scaling an image up, so if you're not positive of the size you want, it's better to scale less than too much (of course, if you really mess up, you can bring the original source image back into the main image again). When you're ready to apply the transformation, press the Return or Enter key.

With every element on its own layer, you can use the Layers palette to hide or view each layer (and element) separately. This will help you to concentrate on the elements you're currently working with and greatly organize the work environment.

To properly scale an image on a layer above to fit an image on a layer below, it can be helpful to see both images simultaneously. One way I do this is to set up the layers temporarily so you can see through the image on top to the main image below (you'll want to reset the layer to be opaque when you no longer need to see both layers at once). To set the top Detail layer so I could see through it to the long shot below, I Targeted the Detail layer in the Layers palette (by clicking on the thumbnail for that layer), and then I changed its default Blending mode from Normal to Multiply, which makes the whites transparent (Figure 1.3). Alternatively, you can reduce the overall opacity of a layer by using the Opacity slider, or if your images are dark, you can try using the Screen Blending mode.

**1.3** After dragging the larger Detail image into the long shot, I made the Detail layer transparent by setting the layer to Multiply mode (sometimes I adjust the Transparency slider as well).

After I could see both images at the same time, I scaled the Detail by clicking its layer and choosing the Free Transform command (Command+T for Mac or Ctrl+T for Windows). By grabbing a corner handle and dragging inward while holding the Shift key down, you will be able to use the Free Transform command to scale down the Detail proportionally.

After nudging the Detail into position and finalizing the transformation, I made a note of the scaling percentages in the Options bar, applied the transformation (by pressing Return), and then used Save As to save the image with the scaled version as a new file (Figure 1.4).

After I scaled the overlaying house Detail, I reset the Blending mode to Normal and Opacity to 100% (Figure 1.5).

**1.4** After targeting the Detail layer, I used the Free Transform command to scale it down proportionally and then nudged the transformation back into position using the arrow cursor keys so I could accurately adjust the final transformation.

**1.5** After I scaled the overlaying house Detail, I reset the Blending mode to Normal and Opacity to 100%.

Although technically there are many ways to approach the process of integrating one image with another, all the projects in this chapter rely on Layer Masks. Layer Masks provide you with a nondestructive way to preserve images intact as you work. Layer Masks control which areas in a layer are visible and which are hidden, which allows you to create the transitions between a layer and the layers below.

To create a Layer Mask for your source image, in the Layers palette first target that layer (by clicking its thumbnail) and then click the Layer Mask icon.

**1.6** After creating a blank Layer Mask for the Detail layer.

After you've added a Layer Mask, you'll see a new thumbnail representing the mask in the Layers palette as well as the new Layer Mask icon next to the Eye icon, which indicates that your layer's mask is active (targeted). To work on a layer, click its thumbnail; to work on a Layer Mask, target the mask thumbnail. By default a blank Layer Mask is white, which allows the entire layer to initially be visible (Figure 1.6).

Layer Masks are attached to individual layers and can contain up to 256 levels of gray (full grayscale). When you add a Layer Mask to your source layer, you'll use black, white, and grays to determine what in the attached layer will be visible and what will be masked (hidden). While white reveals the attached image and black masks it, the range of grays allows you to create semi-transparent effects. You can use your selection tools to select and then fill an area of the Layer Mask, or you can paint directly into the mask with your painting tools to define the subtle boundaries of your mask area. Whether you're using painting tools or selection tools, a graphics tablet is very helpful (maybe essential) to exacting masks (see the Appendix, "Arranging Your Workspace," for more on tablets).

To smooth the transition between my scaled source image and the layer below, I created a Layer Mask for the Detail layer.

You can construct your Layer Mask using a variety of tools. Use your selection tools to select an area and then choose Delete to fill it with the Background color. Press Option (Mac) or Alt (Windows) when you Delete to fill with the Foreground color. See what happens to your source image as you fill areas of that layer with black or white. Pick up a value from your image with the Eyedropper tool or choose a gray from the Colors palette and fill an area of your Layer Mask with that gray. Experiment with the Gradient tool, with both the Linear Gradient and Radial Gradient options, to create Layer Masks that fade from opaque (black) to transparent (white); the Gradient tool creates a smooth transition of colors or values from your Foreground to your Background colors.

NOTE

In your version of Photoshop, the Gradient tool might be hidden beneath another tool in your palette (see your Quick Reference Card for help).

To clear your Layer Mask, Select All (Command+A for Mac or Ctrl+A for Windows) and Delete to white (you might have to reset the default colors, switch Foreground and Background colors, or Delete to the foreground color). To reset the default Foreground color to black and background color to white, press D. To swap the Background and Foreground colors, press X.

I created the Detail Layer Mask, primarily with the Airbrush tool (loaded with either black to mask the Detail layer or white to reveal the Detail layer). I varied the size of the brush to create a mask that revealed the house itself (in white), and softly transitioned (in grays to black) to the Background drawing underneath (Figure 1.7).

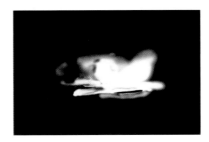

**1.7** The house mask seen as an overlay (with the \ key), just the mask itself, and the resulting composited images.

To get approval from the client, I emailed a flattened JPEG of the composited drawing to her (using Save As then choosing Copy and JPEG as format, to save a flat version). She had two last major requests: that I extend the horizon on the left and that I redraw the foreground shoreline.

In terms of adding more horizon to the left, I looked at my original drawing and discovered that I had drawn but not scanned an extended horizon. My scanner wasn't big enough to fit the entire drawing, so I had just scanned the portion that I thought I'd need at the time. This time I placed the drawing on the scanner bed so it included the full drawing on the left and instead cut off part of the drawing on the right (which I already had in the Background layer). Because I also wanted to straighten out the horizon from the current digital composite, I rotated the drawing slightly on the scanner bed and scanned this version into Photoshop at 300 pixels per inch (Figure 1.8).

**1.8** The scanner was too small to fit the entire drawing, so this time I placed the left side on the bed, slightly rotated it to straighten the horizon, and rescanned at 300 pixels per inch.

Before bringing this new scan into the main image, I needed to increase the canvas size so that there was enough space on the left to accommodate the longer horizon. You can increase your working space by choosing Image> Canvas Size. In Canvas Size, after adding to your canvas size numerically in horizontal and/or vertical dimensions, use the iconic thumbnail to determine where your extra canvas will be added in relationship to your existing image. I added space to the left of my existing image and clicked OK (Figure 1.9).

**1.9** After increasing the canvas size of the main image.

When you patch together elements, you'll need to make sure that all images are not only registered together, but are placed properly within the stacking order of your layers. After using the Move tool to bring the new left horizon drawing into my main image, I used the Move tool also to line up this horizon correctly with the original image below. In the Layers palette, I then dragged this new layer between the Detail and Background layers.

To create the transition between this new version and the Background below, I added a Layer Mask to the Horizon layer. Into this Layer Mask I then used the Linear Gradient tool to blend from white on the left, to black on the right. This Layer Mask revealed the new horizon on the left and revealed the Background (on the layer below) on the right (Figures 1.10 and 1.11).

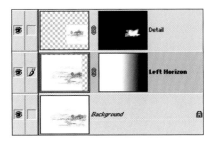

**1.10** The Layers palette showing the Detail, Left Horizon and Background layers, and their masks (shown using the largest thumbnail size in Palette options).

**1.11** The Layer Mask for the Left Horizon layer, shown alone (Shift+click on its Layer Mask thumbnail) and shown with the Layer Mask applied and the Background layer hidden.

To create the new shoreline, instead of redrawing the long shot image (or risk damaging the existing drawing by too much erasure), I overlaid a piece of tracing paper on top of the long shot drawing and redrew only the foreground shoreline (Figure 1.12). Because I was drawing directly on top of the original with the tracing paper, I knew that the scan of this image would fit perfectly in place with the original scan, if scanned at 300 pixels per inch.

**1.12** The redrawn foreground of the shoreline, drawn separately on tracing paper.

After scanning the new shoreline, I used the Move tool to drag and drop this scan into the main image. Making sure that this new shoreline was the topmost layer in the Layers palette, I temporarily set this layer to Multiply so I could see where it should be in position over the images below. After the new shoreline was in position, I created a Layer Mask for this Foreground layer. Into the Layer Mask I used black, grays, and white to create a soft airbrushed transition from this new foreground to the composited drawings below. After a few touch-up corrections (see Chapter 2, "Creative Problem Solving Using Layers"), I ended up with a composited digital image that maintains the character of an original drawing (Figure 1.13).

**1.13** The redrawn foreground of the shoreline in place in the final composited drawing of "The Point."

## Composing in Pieces

If you know ahead of time that you're going to combine images with Photoshop, you can create the parts of a composition separately, knowing that you can put them together later. Planning this from the start can free you up to work more spontaneously and can help you to avoid the stiffness that inevitably occurs when an artist reinterprets an image repeatedly. Just the concept that you will be able to combine images can alter the way you create and collect source material and enhance your creative process.

For over a decade I either created artwork directly on the computer, or I used traditional material to draw and paint. Although in a couple of instances I'd incorporated a scanned drawing into a computer painted image, largely my computer art life was completely separate from my studio art life. However, when I stumbled upon a special translucent drawing paper, my entire digital working process changed completely. The drawing paper that I found is 100% Rag (or Cotton, for archival purposes) and translucent—it is essentially a good quality tracing paper (Bienfang Graphics 360). By using this paper, I began to construct separate drawings that I knew would fit together perfectly in Photoshop (Figure 1.14).

19

Normally, when an artist uses a number of different sources as inspiration to create a composition, she first draws the elements separately, and then creates a master drawing that pulls all of the elements into one composition.

**1.14** The source photos for the series of drawings.

Unfortunately, the process of redrawing the separate elements into one master drawing can often take a number of drawings and redrawings. This process of redrawing elements can often result in stiff master compositions. So for the "Jeff with Cats" image, I decided to use this paper and Photoshop to create the initial drawings separately in such a way that they could be combined to form one master drawing. I drew an overall sketch and then separately drew the studies for each of the elements by overlaying the successive tracing papers on top of the original. Working with the transparency ensured that each separate drawing would fit together perfectly with the other drawings later in Photoshop (Figure 1.15).

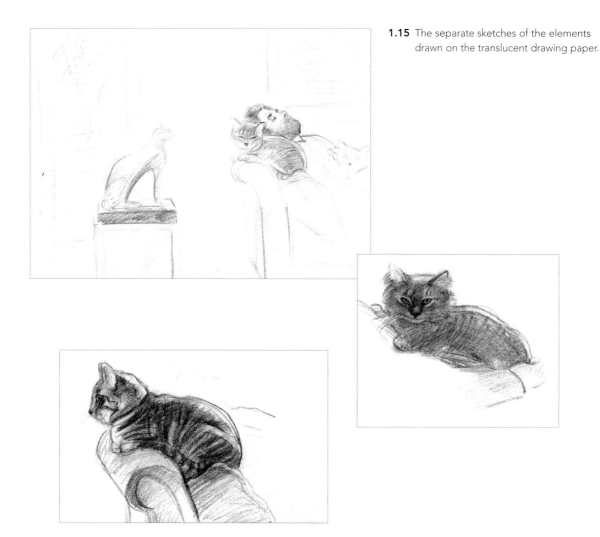

**1.15** The separate sketches of the elements drawn on the translucent drawing paper.

Combine your separate images into one file and move them to their approximate locations within the main file using the Move tool. I scanned each of the drawings separately, using the overall sketch as my main document. For each of the cat detail drawings, I used the Rectangular Marquee to select the portion of the scan with the drawing itself (less white space), copied it, closed the original scan, and pasted it into the Main image. (You also can use the Move tool to drag a selection into another document.) With each newly pasted cat on its own layer, using the Move tool I moved the cats to the correct locations within the main image (remember, they didn't have to be scaled) and saved this file in Photoshop format (Figure 1.16).

**1.16** After the selected portion of the cat image was pasted into the main image.

Sometimes the easiest way to create a Layer Mask is to begin with selection tools. In the case of the "Jeff and the Cats" image, I used selection tools to create the primary Layer Mask and then used painting tools to touch up the mask just a little.

Using the Layers palette, I viewed only the master drawing and one of the cat layers. After deselecting all active selections (Command+D for Mac or Ctrl+D for Windows), I chose the Lasso Selection tool, set the Feather option to 4, and checked Anti-Aliased.

If you have an active selection and don't yet have a Layer Mask, when you click the Layer Mask icon you'll automatically create a mask from your selection. I used the Lasso tool to encircle (thus select) the portion of that image within a layer that I wanted to reveal and then clicked the Layer Mask icon. With the selection active at the time that a Layer Mask is created, the mask automatically reveals the area within the selection and masks the area outside of the selection (Figure 1.17).

At this point I touched up the mask with the Airbrush tool, working into the Layer Mask while viewing just the images (Figure 1.18).

**1.17** One cat selected by the Lasso tool and the resulting mask (shown as an overlay pressing the \ key).

**1.18** After touching up the Layer Mask for the cat, the second figure shows the final Layer Mask as an overlay.

I repeated this process with the other cat to finish the composited master image, as shown in Figure 1.19. (See Chapter 2 for how I did some touch-ups to the final image, and Chapter 3, "Improvising with Color Using Layers," for how I added color to the image.)

**1.19** The composited drawing.

## Seaming a Sequence of Images

Knowing that you can composite images doesn't just affect how you create your source materials—it can inspire you to broaden your conceptions of what you can create.

One example of how compositing allowed me to create something I couldn't do in any other way is the composite of my studio wall. Knowing that I could composite a series of photos inspired me to create a single image that represented my studio wall—an impossible shot using traditional photographic techniques.

I took separate photos of each section of the wall with a 50mm lens (for minimal distortion), overlapping each shot slightly from left to right while trying to maintain the alignment of the shots top-to-bottom as best I could. The ceiling beams interfered with one view or another, but I was able to eliminate the interference of the beams and minimize all distortions when compositing the images in Photoshop. The result of the final Photoshop seamed-together image of my studio wall was not only something I couldn't do in any other way, but couldn't have been done unless I knew ahead of time how I would be combining the photographs (Figure 1.20).

**1.20** The seven snapshots I took for the studio composite and the final composited image of a wall in my studio.

This procedure can be used for any sequence of images, as long as you're careful to give yourself the source information necessary to seam from one image to the next. Collect your source materials and digitize them. I chose to use film for this project (instead of a digital camera), so I began by setting up my camera (with a 50mm lens) on a tripod. I framed the first shot so that enough of the wall was visible top to bottom, which required me to be almost up against the opposite wall. I measured the distance from that opposite wall to my tripod and tried to maintain that distance as I shifted the camera to the right to take the remaining shots. I had my film processed in a lab that created a PhotoCD of my images and returned to me a PhotoCD of my roll of film and a set of mounted slides. I used the digital PhotoCD images to create this studio composite.

If you don't want to process film to PhotoCD, you could scan flat art or shoot directly with a digital camera. After your entire sequence is digitized, you can begin to combine your elements.

Open your main image. Because your other source images will be brought into this main image, you might have to enlarge the canvas size first (Image menu). In Canvas Size you'll use the iconic thumbnail to determine where to add more convas in relation to your existing image. In the case of my studio composite, I used my leftmost image and added blank canvas space to the right and clicked OK. If you don't know how much to add, choose larger than you think you might need and crop it later.

To seam together a sequence of images for each source image in your main file, you'll create a Layer Mask to form a smooth transition to the layer below. After creating a Layer Mask for a Source layer, you'll determine what will be visible in this Source layer and what will be masked (revealing the image below) by working into the Layer Mask with black, whites, and grays. For my studio composite, because my sequence was linear (from left to right), I was able to create Linear gradients in the Layer Mask for each source image to form the basic transitions from one image to the next. Using the Gradient tool (with the Linear option) set to black and white, I created short vertical gradients in the Layer Mask of each section of the studio (hold Shift to constrain a Gradient to horizontal or vertical) to transition from the previous section (below) to that current source shot (Figure 1.21).

When putting the finishing touches on a mask, sometimes it's helpful to see the Layer Mask alone. In the Layers palette, hold down Option (Mac) or Alt (Windows) when you click a Layer Mask thumbnail to view only the mask. Hold Option(Alt) and click again to toggle back to the normal view (the mask is active but not visible). Toggle the Layer Mask on and off (activating and deactivating the mask) by holding the Shift key when you click the Layer Mask icon. Toggle viewing the mask as an overlay with the \ key.

**1.21** The first photo in the studio series, the second photo placed on top is next shown with its linear gradient Layer Mask as an overlay, and then the first two images in position with the Layer Mask applied.

You can move any layer around by activating it first and then using the Move tool. You also can move more than one layer together as a unit by *linking* layers. To link layers, click one of the layers in the Layers palette to activate it and then click in the column next to the Eye for any other layer that you want to link to the first. As long as the links are visible, using the Move tool with any of these active (and unlocked) layers will move the others as well.

In between a layer thumbnail and its mask is also a Link icon thumbnail indicating that a Layer Mask is linked to its image. When you use the Move tool on a linked layer or its mask, you'll move both. To move a Layer Mask independently from its image, hide the Layer Mask Link icon. While they are unlinked, using the Move tool allows you to separately adjust the position of the Layer Mask or the layer, but don't forget to relink them when you're done!

After final touchups (see Chapter 2), I had created a full frontal shot of my studio wall, which would have been impossible in one photographic shot (Figure 1.22).

**1.22** The final composited photo of my south studio wall.

## More Exploration Suggestions

If you are already working on an image that requires additional source input, you don't necessarily have to begin all over again, redraw, or reshoot the entire image. Try instead to create additional drawings or take additional photos and incorporate the additional sources digitally into the existing version.

Shoot a series of photos of a landscape or a building knowing that you will seam them together later in Photoshop. Try experimenting with different focal lengths of the lens or perspectives in the drawings to see how distortion affects your ability to seam things together.

Draw or photograph a series of images planning to piece together parts of each later. If you are drawing, try to work with tracing paper to create drawings that will fit together when scanned and masked. If you're photographing, use a tripod and shoot a series of photographs of moving targets (that is, a flock of birds or a flow of traffic). Plan on assembling parts of different photographs from the same vantage point to create a new whole.

Experiment with Layer Masks using the following:

- Various Selection tools and deleting to fill large areas of color.

- Linear or Radial Gradients to create soft transitions.

- Painting tools to make "cookie cutter" masks.

- An active selection that is automatically turned into a Layer Mask.

- Different ways to view a Layer Mask—alone, as an overlay, or the image without the layer.

CHAPTER 2

# Creative Problem Solving Using Layers

If you always do everything perfectly the first time and never change your mind, then you won't need this chapter. Of course things often go wrong. We change our minds, and the project often changes in direction; but nothing challenges you more to think creatively than having to fix what went wrong.

There's rarely only one right way to do anything in Photoshop. If you gave a group of Photoshop experts a set of problems to solve, they'd probably come up with completely different solutions. I'll often solve a similar problem differently from one day to the next.

So when things don't go as planned, try to focus on each problem as a creative challenge. If you can make this Zen adjustment of attitude, in which you are always in pursuit of finding what kinds of things are possible, then you might even enjoy the process of clean-up and correction.

Detail of before and after unifying color and value, cleaning up blurred and double-image, and patching up image holes.

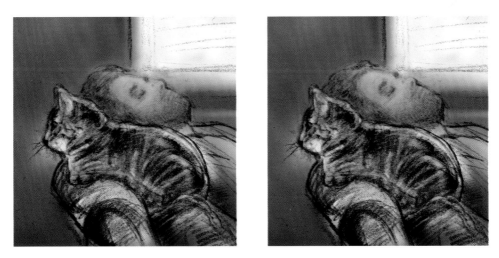

Detail of before and after enlarging Jeff's head and integrating it with the remaining image.

In this chapter, I'll be resolving a range of common clean-up issues (primarily on images detailed in other chapters) regarding layers, adjustment layers, and Layer Masks. Although the structure of the chapter might give the illusion that I progress sequentially throughout a project, this is far from the truth. Much of the time I jump around from issue to issue and often will return to something and fix a problem that I thought I had resolved earlier.

Again, I want to remind you not to focus on the specifics of these projects or how I solved a certain set of problems. The most important thing is for you to envision how finding solutions can be an integral part of your creative process.

## Last Minute Scaling

I strongly recommend that you avoid scaling anything larger in Photoshop; when you scale things up, they can become fuzzy as a result of Photoshop guessing how to add pixels. However, the practical reality is that you can usually get away with scaling things up *a little*.

This image of "Jeff and the Cats" was begun by compositing three drawings in Photoshop (see Chapter 1, "Compositing and the Creative Process," for details). I then created what I thought was a final colored version of the image using techniques discussed in Chapter 3, "Improvising with Color Using Layers."

While looking at a proof of this image, someone pointed out to me that Jeff's head was too small, or the cats were too big (Figure 2.1).

So I decided to scale up Jeff's head. Because the file was multi-layered at this point, Jeff's head actually existed on multiple layers. You can save a flattened version of a layered file in TIFF format and then open and scale the flat version.

Alternatively you can scale a flat copy of a layered file. Make your selection (or Edit> Select All) and then choose Edit> Copy Merged (Command+Shift+C for Mac or Ctrl+Shift+C for Windows). To place this copy into a new layer, click the layer you want it to be pasted above and paste it. For Jeff's head I used the Lasso tool to select the area around the head, set the Feathering to 3, and chose Copy Merged.

I then clicked on the top layer in the Layers palette and pasted this merged copy. The new layer with just Jeff's head was now the top-most layer (Figure 2.2).

One way to scale the contents of a layer, if it's not the active layer, is to click it in the Layers palette and then choose the Free Transform command (Command+T for Mac or Ctrl+T for Windows). You can adjust the size of the active transformation from any handle (to scale up a layer proportionately, grab a corner handle, and drag outward while holding the Shift key down). To rotate the selection, move your cursor outside of a corner until you see the Rotate icon and then click-drag to rotate.

**2.1** In this original final version, Jeff's head was too small.

**2.2** After selecting and copying Jeff's head, I pasted it, which placed the head into its own layer.

I used the Free Transform command and then grabbed the upper-left corner to enlarge Jeff's head slightly, while keeping it attached to his neck on the lower right (Figure 2.3).

If you need to, you can create a Layer Mask for this scaled layer and soften the transition between the enlarged area and the rest of the image on the layer below. To blend Jeff's new head into the image, I created a Layer Mask for the Head layer by clicking the Layer Mask icon in the Layers palette. I then used the Paintbrush tool to paint into the Layer Mask to hide portions of the layer I didn't want using black and using white (or the eraser if white is the Background color) to make corrections to my mask (Figure 2.4).

I saved a copy of the final version as a flattened TIFF file for easy placement into a page layout program.

**2.3** Scaling Jeff's head a little bit larger using the Free Transform command.

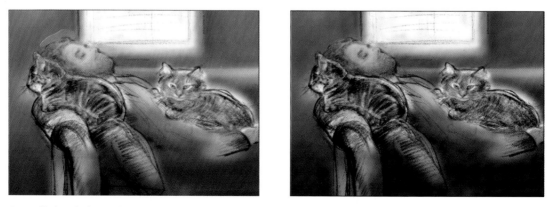

**2.4** Jeff's head after scaling, the mask for the Head layer (shown as an overlay using the \ key), and the final head shown cropped.

## Touching Up Darks and Lights and Equalizing Value

In Chapter 1, I covered how I created a digital drawing of a client's house (called "The Point") by compositing four drawings together. After the client approved the composition however, I needed to clean up the final version to my satisfaction (Figure 2.5).

**2.5** The image of "The Point" as approved by the client, but before my final cleanups.

### Touching Up the Darks and Lights

The first touch-ups that I wanted to focus on were punching up some darks and cleaning up the whites. To create the darks, I made a new layer above the composited image by clicking the New Layer icon in the Layers palette. In the Layers palette, I then set this layer to the Multiply Blending mode so the new marks would interact with the drawing underneath and therefore maintain much of the texture. So that I could draw subtlely with my graphics tablet, I used a small Brush tool with the Brush Dynamics option set to be pressure sensitive in Size and Opacity (see the Appendix, "Arranging Your Workspace," for more about tablets). Using black and almost black colors, I lightly and slowly drew in the areas where I wanted to create more darks, undoing and using the Eraser tool as needed (you can use the Eraser portion of the Stylus if you're using a tablet). See Figure 2.6.

**2.6** Punching black into the composition on a New Layer set to Multiply Blending mode.

To clean up the whites, I created another new layer on top of the others. Into this top layer I painted with white using the painting tools and erasing my marks as needed.

### Equalizing Value

To finish the image, I needed to equalize the value between the detail of the house itself (which was drawn and then composited separately) with the rest of the composition.

Special layers called *Adjustment Layers* provide you with many ways to alter the colors and values of your image. In the Layers palette, click and hold the Adjustment Layer icon to see the long list of options.

While some of the options, such as Gradient, Pattern, and Posterize, create layers that radically shift your image, most of the options provide you with powerful ways to make more subtle adjustments. Experiment with the different options for adjusting your image (refer to your Photoshop manual if you need help figuring it out).

In this project I used the Layer Mask attached to the Adjustment Layer to control how the adjustment would be applied.

If you have an active selection when you create a new Adjustment Layer, your selection is automatically transformed into the Layer Mask for that

Adjustment Layer. This Layer Mask reveals your adjustments within the area you had selected and will protect the area outside your selection from your adjustments.

For "The Point" I decided that I wanted to shift the value of the majority of the image to match the slightly darker value of the house Detail. To adjust everything *except* the Detail, I began by selecting the Detail of the house with the Lasso tool and then chose Select> Inverse. When I chose Levels from the Adjustment Layer icon in the Layers palette, the Adjustment Layer Mask affected everything except the house (Figure 2.7).

**2.7** After selecting the house Detail, I chose Select> Inverse to select everything but the Detail.

With everything active except the Detail layer, I chose Levels from the Adjustment Layer icon in the Layers palette. The portion of your image, which was selected when you created a new Adjustment Layer, is the portion you'll be adjusting. You'll soften the transition between this adjustment and the rest of your image later, so concentrate on the basic correction. In the Levels dialog box I darkened the portion of the image that had been selected (moving the center slider slightly to the right) and clicked OK. I then used my Brush tool, using black and white to clean up the mask for the Adjustment Layer so that the transition between the house and the rest of the image was smooth (Figure 2.8).

The last decision I made after applying the darker Adjustment Layer to the composition was to tone down the blacks somewhat by setting the Opacity of the layer to 59% (Figure 2.9).

**2.8** The cleaned up Layer Mask for the house (shown as an overlay by clicking the mask in the Channels palette), and the Adjustment Layer and Mask as they appeared in the Layers palette.

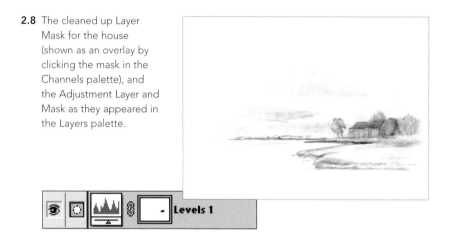

**2.9** The final, cleaned-up version of "The Point."

## Unifying Color and Patching Together Missing Pieces

I covered the basics of compositing this single image from seven digitized photos in Chapter 1 (Figure 2.10). As it turns out, the reality of repairing what went wrong in the process was by far the most time-consuming part of project.

**2.10** The rough composite of the studio after I'd created basic vertical gradient Layer Masks but before other touch-ups, and the final studio after touch-ups.

Using a 35mm camera on a tripod and a 50mm lens, I intended to take a sequence of shots that kept the same framing top to bottom. As I moved from left to right, I wanted to overlap each picture with the previous shot and get a shot of each column of paintings centered in the frame. Additionally, I wanted to take two versions of each shot, one with natural light only and with daylight-light bulbs boosting the light.

I stood with my back up against the opposite wall and framed the first shot. I measured the distance from my rear tripod leg to the wall and made note as to what was in the top and bottom, left and right of my frame. I took a shot, crossed the room to turn on the daylight bulbs (to boost the natural light), and took the second shot. I'd then reset the lights, move over the tripod, and take the next shot. Needless to say, this was an imperfect way to proceed. When I got my PhotoCD back from the lab along with the mounted slides, I found a variety of problems. First, although I had intended each framing of a shot to be exposed with daylight alone and with the boost of lights, I had unintentionally missed a few shots. As a result, some of the shots were taken with just daylight, others with just the boosting light, so I couldn't just choose one consistent lighting style to use. The next problem was that I'd forgotten to center one column of paintings in frame (starting with the green apples at the top). Though I did at least have these paintings at the edges of the shots to the left and right of the missed column of pictures, the missing shot would make it a bit more difficult to line up the transition from one shot to the next. Lastly, and not surprisingly, the horizontal framing of the sequence bobbed up and down just enough to create gaps in the framing of the overall composite. I'll cover how I solved each of these issues separately, along with some other issues that popped up along the way.

## Unifying the Color Balance of Separate Shots

After compositing the images together, the Photoshop file contained seven separate layers. The bottom layer was the leftmost shot, with each consecutive shot in the layer above. Each layer, except the original Background layer, had a Layer Mask attached to it, which helped to form the basic transitions between one shot and the shot below it. Each Layer Mask contained a black-to-white vertical Linear Gradient that revealed (black) the image below and then gradually transitioned to reveal (white) the attached layer (Figure 2.11). (For more details on this process, please see Chapter 1.)

If you simply create a new Adjustment Layer, that adjustment will affect all layers that are positioned below it. However, you also can create Adjustment Layers that are attached to and affect only the specific layer directly below it. To create an Adjustment Layer that is automatically attached to the currently active layer, hold down the Option key (Mac) or Alt key (Windows) while you choose a New Adjustment Layer from the Layers palette (such as Levels, Curves, and so on). In the dialog box, check the Group With Previous Layer option and click OK. When you enable this, the Adjustment Layer will affect only the layer that was currently active when you created the layer. Then you can make adjustments that will apply to only the layer below it and click OK when you're satisfied. You'll notice that in the Layers palette, an arrow that points down indicates that an Adjustment Layer is grouped with the layer below (Figure 2.12).

For this studio composite, to blend in color and value with the layer below it, each layer needed its own Adjustment Layer. Starting from the Background layer, I created a Levels Adjustment Layer, holding down Option to group it with that layer and made the Levels adjustment to that layer. Then I moved to the next layer and created a new Adjustment layer for it (Figure 2.13). Sometimes I'd toggle the Layer Mask off (Shift+click on the Layer Mask icon) to better see the effects of the adjustment.

**2.11** The Layers palette with each of the shots on its own layer. Attached to each layer is a Layer Mask containing a vertical Linear Gradient that creates the transition from that layer to the layer below.

**2.12** In the Layers palette, the Background layer is shown first with an Adjustment Layer grouped to it.

**2.13** A section of the studio composite is shown first with the Layer Masks hidden, then active, and finally after I'd applied the Adjustment Layers to each layer.

Layers 5–7 required a similar adjustment to the one that I had created for Layer 4. Instead of creating new Adjustment Layers for each of these layers, I duplicated the Adjustment Layer for Layer 4 (by dragging the icon over the New Layer icon in the Layers palette). I then dragged the duplicate into position above the next layer that needed that adjustment. To manually group this moved layer with its new Adjustment Layer, in the Layers palette, hold Option (for Mac) or Alt (for Windows) and click the line between the two layers (Figure 2.14). You can detach an Adjustment Layer from the layer it's been grouped with by holding Option (Mac) or Alt (Windows) and clicking again on the line in the Layers palette that separates an Adjustment Layer from the layer below.

As always, you can create Adjustment Layers that apply to all layers below the adjustment (and not just the layer directly below it). To lighten up the very bottom section of the entire image, I first activated the topmost layer in the Layers palette. Next, I used the Rectangular Marquee tool to select a strip along the bottom of the entire composition. Then I created a New Adjustment Layer and chose Levels so I could then lighten the selected area by moving the center slider to the left and clicked OK. Into this Layer Mask for the new Adjustment Layer, I then used the Linear Gradient tool to replace the temporary rectangular mask with a black-to-white horizontal gradient, smoothing the transition from this lightened adjustment to the rest of the image (Figure 2.15).

**NOTE**
You can connect any two layers by clicking the line between the layers while holding down Option(Alt), but connecting layers can create different results, such as Clipping Groups (depending on what type of layers you are connecting).

**2.14** The Layers palette for the studio shown after I created the Adjustment Layers. For Layers 5–7 I duplicated the Adjustment for Layer 4 (by dragging it over the New Layer icon), moved it into position, and then manually grouped it with the layer below by clicking the line between them in the Layers palette while holding down Option(Alt).

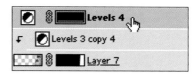

**2.15** The Layers palette showing the horizontal strip lightening up the bottom of the entire image.

### Refining Transitions in the Layer Masks

It would be great if Linear Gradient masks created smooth transitions from one image to another, but the reality of this is that for most projects, such transitions need to be manually modified. The vertical Linear Gradients did a perfectly fine job creating transitions for most of the shots of flat paintings against a flat wall. However, there were blurred and double images where the images weren't in perfect alignment from one shot to the next. This was most evident where the gradients couldn't be placed in areas between objects, such as in the column of paintings missing the straight-on shot and with the three-dimensional objects such as the carts. To eliminate the blurred and double images, I needed to manually clean up the transitions in the Layer Masks. With so many layers, to determine which layers were creating double images, I would hide all layers except the Background (click the Eye icon to hide or show a layer) and then click the Eye to show the next layer. If that layer were a culprit, I'd target its Layer Mask (by clicking its thumbnail).

The blurred and double images were occurring in areas where the Layer Mask was semi-transparent, while the current layer and the layer below were not in perfect registration (Figure 2.16). To fix the blurring, I had to replace the transparency in those areas with opaque areas of white (to reveal the current layer) or black (to reveal the image below). I used the painting tools to paint with opaque black and white, figuring out as I painted which layer worked better in the current area (Figure 2.17). (Pressing the X key swaps the Foreground and Background colors.) While I worked, I'd periodically view the mask alone to see if it needed cleaning up (Shift+click on the Layer Mask icon) as well as viewed the mask as an overlay (the \ key toggles the Overlay mode on and off).

### Patching Up Gaps and Holes

After equalizing the color and value of the image and eliminating blurred and double-images, I had another major problem to contend with. Although I had tried very hard to maintain top-to-bottom registration as I photographed the studio wall, I had bobbed up and down just enough to create some gaps in the image. The easiest solution would have been to simply crop the image to the area that was intact. However, that would have meant losing a few paintings that I wanted to keep in the composition. In some instances I could have re-shot the scene, but this would have been more time-consuming than just faking it in those missing areas. Depending on what the image looked like in a problem area, I used different techniques to fill the gaps, including moving copies of portions of the image down or up, stretching regions to fill gaps, and using the Clone Stamp tool to copy portions from another section of the image.

**2.16** A detail of the studio showing a double image, and the original Linear Gradient mask for that area.

**2.17** The same detail with the mask cleaned up, and the cleaned-up mask shown alone.

In a few instances, I decided to stretch a copy of a portion of the image to fill the gap in it. I'd first select the area that I wanted to stretch. Sometimes I'd need to hide some layers before I copied the area. Most of the time, the area that I wanted to expand existed on multiple layers, so I couldn't simply use the Copy command. To copy a selection that covers multiple layers, make sure that you have a visible layer active, choose Edit> Copy Merged (Command+Shift+C for Mac, Ctrl+Shift+C for Windows), and then select Paste to place a copy of the merged area into its own layer. Once the copy exists on its own layer, you can choose Edit> Transform (Command+T for Mac, Ctrl+T for Windows).

I started by stretching copies to fill the gaps (Figure 2.18). In the case of the orange area, I only needed to stretch it down, while in other instances I needed to enlarge the copy in a number of dimensions. When I was satisfied, I clicked OK.

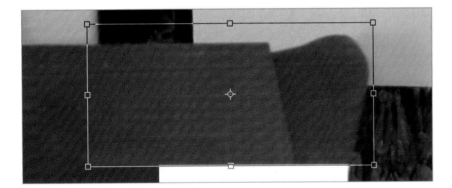

**2.18** Stretching the transformation down to fill the gap (I needed to enlarge the copy slightly taller from the top as well), and the copy after the transformation was applied.

Throughout the reparation of this image, I used a variety of different patching methods, including the Clone Stamp tool, which I used to clone part of an image or a texture from one area to another. Before cloning, I'd always start by creating a new layer above the existing one (by clicking the New Layer icon). With this new layer active, I'd then use the Clone Stamp to clone into the new layer, using the Use All Layers option.

Before you can clone from one area to another with the Clone Stamp tool, you have to define the area that you are cloning. Hold the Option key (Mac) or Alt key (Windows) and click to define the area you want to clone and then move your cursor to the area from where you would like to re-create the original and start drawing. For more precision in locating where the clone starts or begins, press the Caps Lock key, which will change your cursor into a crosshair, the center of the crosshair being your exact location. When you want to copy a larger area to another location (like I did to clone the shadow from under one of my paintings to under another painting) use the Aligned option; as you draw you'll continue to align the clone to the original until you tell it otherwise.

In areas where you want to clone texture (such as patching in an area of the wall), disable the Aligned option so that each time you begin to draw you'll re-reference the original starting point. Use the Aligned option to redraw something specific, such the right ceiling beam to replace the left one. Whenever you use the Clone Stamp tool, I highly recommend that you work in a blank new layer, above the rest of your image so that you don't affect the actual image itself.

**NOTE**

To draw lines with any tool (including the Clone Stamp tool), click where you want the line to begin, hold down the Shift key, and click to connect your first mark with a line.

Sometimes the simplest solution is best. In patching the area around my studio cart, I first selected an area, chose Edit> Copy Merged, and pasted it into its own layer. I first tried to stretch the area above to cover the blank space below, but when I was unhappy with the stretched painting, I deleted that layer and started over. Instead I pasted another copy on top into its own layer and simply moved it down to cover the blank space. To blend the copy with the version below, I created a Layer Mask for the copy and used painting tools to soften the transition between the layers (Figure 2.19).

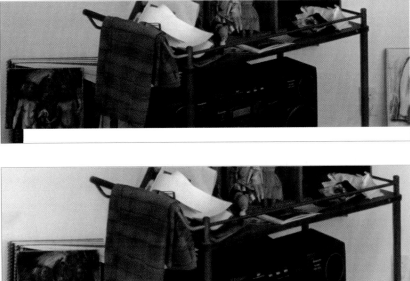

**2.19** Before and after patching the area around my studio cart.

## More Exploration Suggestions

Experiment with different ways to change the color or value of an area of your image using Adjustment Layers (Levels, Curves, Hue/Saturation, and so on) and then try different ways to isolate the area, such as the following:

- Select an area, copy and paste (using Copy Merged if necessary), and create an Adjustment Layer that is grouped with the copy by holding Option (Mac) or Alt (Windows) when you create the Adjustment Layer.

- Select an area and create an Adjustment Layer for that selection using its Layer Mask.

- Select an area, Invert the selection (Select> Inverse), and create an Adjustment Layer for that selection using its Layer Mask.

- Select an area, create an Adjustment Layer for that selection using its Layer Mask, and then invert the Layer Mask (Command+I for Mac, Ctrl+I for Windows).

The next few times you need to clean up an image, try to use these different methods:

- Duplicate a layer, apply a filter, hold Option (Mac) or Alt (Windows) when you create a Layer Mask, and then paint in the filtered area using white in your Layer Mask.

- Make an Adjustment Layer and lighten or darken the image, then reverse the Adjustment Layer Mask, and paint into the Mask with white to reveal the adjustment.

- In a new, blank layer above your image, use the Clone Stamp tool to clone good areas of your image over problem ones. To make corrections, re-clone, erase, or attach a Layer Mask to this clone layer to paint out areas you choose.

- Place layers above an image so that you can touch up lights and darks. To touch up lights, set the Layer Blending mode to Screen or Normal. To touch up darks, set the Layer Blending mode to Multiply or Normal. Try different blending modes on each of the touch-up layers.

- Try patching holes in an image by stretching, moving, and cloning areas from elsewhere in the image into new layers above the original.

CHAPTER 3

# Improvising with Color Using Layers

This chapter uses color layers to transform images, starting predictably with adding color and ending with improvisational explorations in color and texture. After you begin experimenting and improvising with your own photographic or drawn images, you'll discover how magical it can be to invite Photoshop to participate in your creative process.

One of the most exciting things for me as an artist is that Photoshop allows me to develop a final composition from drawings without sacrificing the initial spontaneity of the sketch or drawing. In the past, after creating drawings or sketches, artists would then need to develop ideas from the sketch into a broader composition or more completed version. However, by continually redrawing or by mechanically transferring a drawing to another medium (such as transferring a compositional drawing to a canvas or fresco wall), it's easy to lose the spontaneity of an original inspiration.

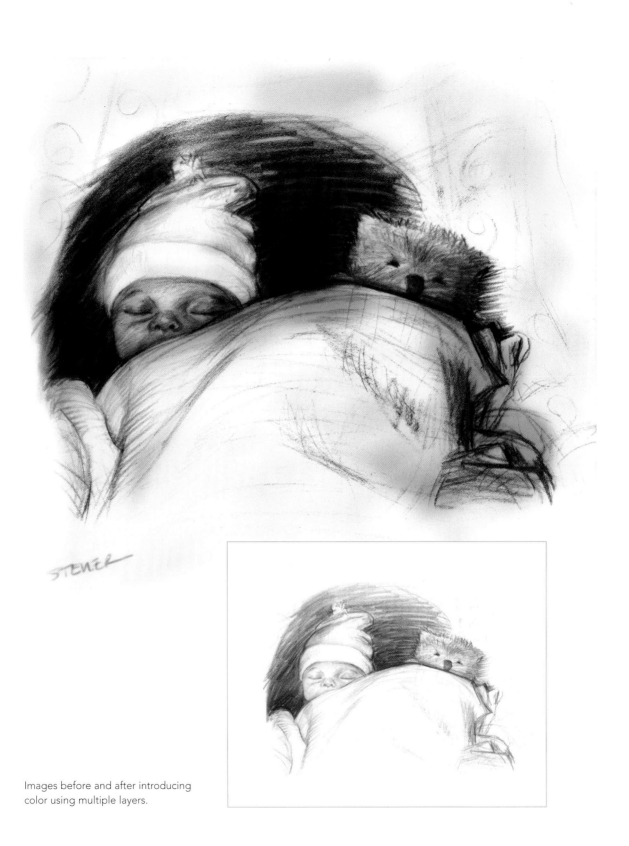

Images before and after introducing
color using multiple layers.

It's important to understand that I rarely know exactly what I want the finished image to look like, and I never know exactly how many layers I'll end up with—or what modes those layers will be set to. The only rule of thumb that I do adhere to is: Whenever I see an effect that I like, I create a new layer so I can freely experiment from that point forward, while easily being able to get back to the last point I liked. To repeat an effect elsewhere, I note then replicate the specific configuration of layers.

By experimenting with duplicating layers of color, Photoshop can do more for you than merely allow you to color images. Working in this way, Photoshop can help you generate ideas, add elements of creative improvisation to the way you work, and help you to achieve completely unexpected artistic results.

## Basic Coloring with Layers

For the first decade I created art on the computer, I almost never incorporated traditionally created drawings or paintings into my digital images.

This all changed when Photoshop introduced Blending modes for layers. With this portrait of Maia and Puma, I began to experiment with introducing color to black and white images (see Figure 3.1). I scanned the drawing in as grayscale and saved it as a TIFF.

To add color to a black and white image, the first thing that you need to do is change the color space for the file from grayscale to either RGB or CMYK. Choose the RGB or CMYK color space from the Image> Mode menu.

In the Layers palette, the default Blending mode for layers is Normal. A simple way to add color to a black and white image is to start by creating a new layer above the image by clicking the New Layer icon (Option[Alt] and click the Create New Layer icon to name the layer as you create it). Next, in the Layers palette, change the Blending mode for the new blank layer to Multiply. When in Multiply mode, your colors won't mask your image below but will instead blend with the image. You'll be able to paint over the white and light areas, while preserving the blacks and the texture underneath. For this portrait I used the painting tools to paint colors into the layer set to Multiply mode (Figure 3.2).

But this looked too flat, and the black lines of the drawing appeared actually too intact. To lighten areas of an image, place another blank layer above the Multiply layer and set it to Screen. With the upper layer set to Screen mode, I was able to gradually paint in highlights, as well as corrections to the drawing, as if I were painting with light (Figure 3.3).

**3.1** The original drawing as scanned in grayscale.

**3.2** To add the basic color to the image, I painted into a new layer set to Multiply Blending mode.

**3.3** To lighten areas I painted into a new layer set to Screen mode (also shown is the Layers palette for the image and the layers above).

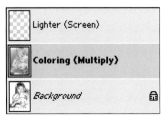

To make final corrections to the image (such as lightening the background), I added an additional layer set to Normal mode. Working into this Normal layer, I could cover up anything in the layers below with opaque color and the painting tools (Figure 3.4).

**3.4** The final portrait of Maia and Puma.

## Experimenting with Layers and Blending Modes

Knowing that I could add color to images allowed me to begin thinking outside the box. After I combined separate sketches to form a final rough composition in Photoshop (see Chapter 1, "Compositing and the Creative Process," for details), I applied colors using layers. I began the following example much like the previous project, changing the color mode of the grayscale scan to RGB and then adding a Multiply mode layer on top. In the Multiply mode layer I flushed out some basic colors using the painting tools (Figures 3.5 and 3.6).

Just for the heck of it, I began to experiment with changing the color mode of this color layer. When I got to Color Burn, I stopped—this was something I'd never seen before. Rather than just overlaying color onto a drawing, the color transformed the strokes themselves, creating an almost colored pencil effect (Figure 3.7).

**3.5** The original composited grayscale image.

**3.6** After converting the image to RGB, I created a new layer, set it to Multiply mode, and painted my basic colors into that layer.

**3.7** Changing the Multiply mode layer to Color Burn, placed the color within the strokes of the drawing.

**3.8** Duplicating the Color Burn layer intensified the effect.

Next, I duplicated the Color Burn layer (by dragging the layer over the New Layer icon in the Layers palette) and noticed that the effect was intensified (Figure 3.8).

To place the color into the white areas of the image, I duplicated the layer again, moved it above the others (select and drag it by its name into the Layers palette), and set the new duplicate to Multiply mode (Figures 3.9 and 3.10).

**3.9** The image and Layers palette after duplicating the layer again—I moved it above the other layers and set it to Multiply.

**3.10** Converting the image to RGB, I created a new layer, set it to Multiply mode, and painted into that layer my basic colors.

The newest Multiply mode layer was too dark in spots. To lessen the Multiply effect in selective areas, I attached a Layer Mask to the Multiply mode layer by clicking the Layer Mask icon in the Layers palette. In areas where I wanted to reduce the effect, I used black and grays to paint into the Layer Mask with the painting tools (Figure 3.11). To bring back the effect, use the Eraser or paint with light grays or white. (For more details about Layer Masks see Chapter 1.)

This Multiply layer didn't look quite right at full opacity, but it lost much of the richness when lightened to 61% Opacity, so I tried duplicating the Multiply layer (including its Layer Mask). Setting the Opacity of the duplicate to 100% made it look dark but not as dark as the single layer set to 100% (Figure 3.12).

**3.11** The Layer Mask for the Multiply Mask as seen alone (by selecting Option[Alt] and clicking on the Mask icon in the Layers palette), and how the image looked with that mask applied.

**3.12** After duplicating the Multiply layer with mask.

Because it was still too dark, I gradually adjusted the Opacity of the duplicated Multiply layer until I got something I liked (at 71%). Somehow, because of how Multiply mode technically works, the two layers set to 61% and 70% resulted in colors less intense and dark than the one Multiply mode set to 100%. Through pure experimentation, I found that if you duplicate a layer and adjust the Opacity of the duplicate, you can achieve different results than is possible with one layer alone.

To lighten areas of the image (mostly the eyes of the cats), I created a layer on top set to Screen mode then painted into that layer with light colors. And lastly I scaled up Jeff's head just a little as shown in Figure 3.13 (see Chapter 2, "Creative Problem Solving Using Layers," for details).

**3.13**  The final image after touch-ups, and the final layer structure.

## Planned Improvisations with Color

Knowing that you can add color to images and seeing how different color modes can substantially change the character of images should encourage you to create work that can later be colored in Photoshop. But this way of working can do more than just allow you to add color to images. You can use this way of working to expand your approach to creating images by continuing to experiment with different ways to add richness, as well as color, to your images. Working with the "Baby and the Bear" image was the first time that I decided to allow the computer to suggest creative directions for the development of an image.

I drew a portrait of my friend's child and her toy bear with a brown pencil on soft cotton paper (Figure 3.14).

I scanned it into Photoshop as grayscale to convert the browns to blacks. To begin the coloring process, I changed the color mode to RGB (Image> Mode> RGB). I started out much as before by creating a new layer, setting that layer to Multiply mode, and coloring into the Multiply layer with painting tools (Figure 3.15).

**3.14** The original brown pencil drawing.

**3.15** The image after painting into a new Multiply mode colors layer.

After the basic colors were flushed out, I was ready to start experimenting to see how I wanted those colors applied and see what effect I actually wanted to achieve.

I began by experimenting with changing the Multiply mode layer to other Blending modes in the Layers palette. Though a different effect than Color Burn, the Soft Light mode is another Blending mode that places color into darks. With this grayscale drawing, Soft Light placed color into the strokes themselves (Figure 3.16).

At this point I began a series of experimental steps, starting with duplicating this first colored layer and then duplicating the Soft Light layer again (Figure 3.17).

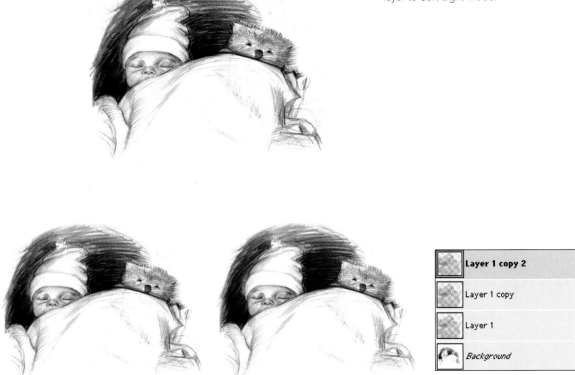

**3.16** Experimenting with different Blending modes, I changed the Multiply mode layer to Soft Light mode.

**3.17** After duplicating the Soft Light layer, and then duplicating it again.

To add some richness to the colors, I experimented with trying different blending modes and adjusting the Opacity until I settled on Hard Light with a 54% Opacity (Figure 3.18). With so many duplicate layers, I decided to start naming each layer meaningfully by double-clicking each layer name and typing a new name (in some versions of Photoshop, you'll need to hold Option[Alt] when double-clicking).

I duplicated the color layer one more time, and this time I tried the Color Dodge Blending mode. This flooded the image with a bleached light that I liked, but it also obliterated much of the image. I reduced the Opacity of the Color Dodge layer gradually, deciding on 5% Opacity. This gave me a very subtle (almost imperceptible) boost of the highlights (Figure 3.19).

**3.18** After duplicating the color layer again and setting it to Hard Light mode at 54%, and the Layers palette after customizing the layer names.

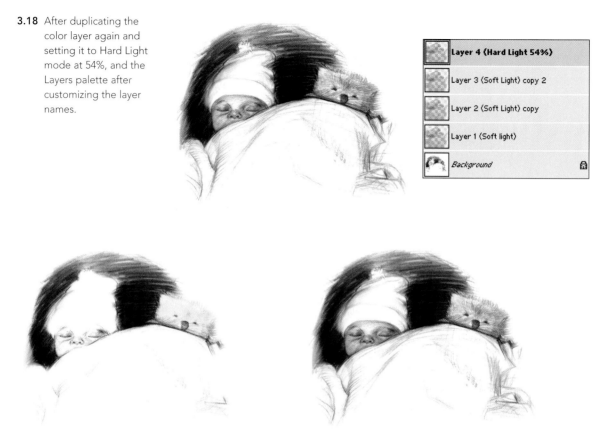

Layer 4 (Hard Light 54%)

Layer 3 (Soft Light) copy 2

Layer 2 (Soft Light) copy

Layer 1 (Soft light)

*Background*

**3.19** After adding a Color Dodge layer, and then reducing the Opacity down to (a very subtle) 5%.

After adding six color layers, I was losing some of the original detail of the image, so I duplicated the original Background layer, moved it above the color layers, and set it to Multiply mode (Figure 3.20). To control where the blacks were made richer, I created a Layer Mask for the copy of the background (by clicking the Layer Mask icon) and painted into the mask using black, white, grays, and painting tools (Figure 3.21).

At this point most of the color was still just within the lines themselves, so I created another duplicate of the color layer. After moving this duplicate on top of the other layers, I set it to Multiply mode and adjusted the Opacity to 33% (Figure 3.22).

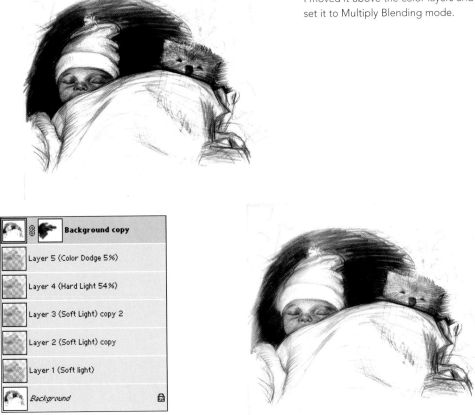

**3.20** After duplicating the Background layer, I moved it above the color layers and set it to Multiply Blending mode.

**3.21** Attaching a Layer Mask to the Multiply layer, I painted into the Layer Mask to control where the Multiply was applied.

**3.22** To add overall color to the image, I duplicated the color layer again, setting this one to Multiply mode at 33% Opacity.

I wanted richer colors in some areas so I duplicated the Multiply color layer and created a Layer Mask for the duplicate. By painting into that Layer Mask I was able to control where the richer colors were actually applied (Figure 3.23).

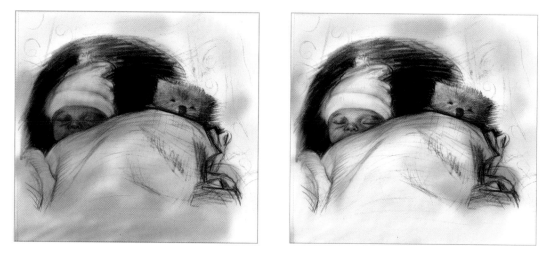

**3.23** After creating a Layer Mask so I could control where the Multiply was applied.

After duplicating this last color layer with the Layer Mask, I adjusted the Opacity and painted into the mask, altering how this Multiply layer would be applied. Finally, I added a blank new layer on top of all the others so that I could paint with the painting and Clone Stamp tools for some simple touch-up corrections (Figure 3.24). (For more about touch-up layers, see Chapter 2.)

**NOTE**

In earlier versions of Photoshop, saving in TIFF format automatically created files without layers or Alpha channels; in newer versions you might have to manually choose to exclude layers/ channels to create a flattened TIFF file.

I thought the image might be complete, so I saved a flat version by using Save As and choosing TIFF. Opening this flat version, I realized that I had forgotten to add a signature. I added a signature, did some last minute touchups on a new layer above, and then saved a flattened version of this image. Wanting a bit more texture to the image, I applied Filter> Artistic> Rough Pastels and played around with the various options until I got something I liked (Figure 3.25).

To finish the image, I combined the pastel version with the non-pastel version. With both images open and visible, I used the Move tool to drag the pastel version into the file with the non-pastel flattened version, holding down the Shift key to align the images.

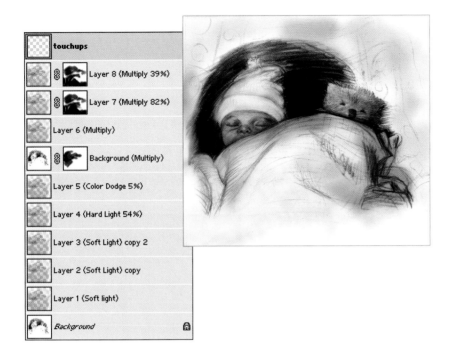

**3.24** The image after touch-ups, and the Layers palette at this stage.

**3.25** After applying the Rough Pastels filter to a flattened version of the image.

After they were together in one file, I reduced the Opacity on the pastel version (now on its own layer) so that it blended with the version underneath (44%). Finally, I wanted to brighten up the light in the image, so I duplicated the background, non-pastel color layer and moved it above the pastel layer. Playing around with various layer modes, I chose Soft Light and reduced the Opacity to 57%. To tone down the effect in some spots, I added a Layer Mask to this top layer and selectively painted out the effect (Figure 3.26).

**3.26** The final image and Layers palette for the final version of the image.

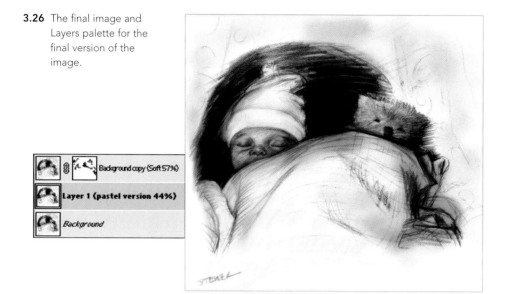

## Continued Improvisations with Color

You can use this improvisational process to enrich and transform a wide variety of images.

In many cases I'll play with readjusting Blending modes and Opacities of individual layers as I work. I'll continue to add or work within Layer Masks and also reorder some of the layers, which can often completely change the overall effect. See Chapter 5, "Nonlinear Creativity," for examples of even less methodical working processes.

The specific details of Blending modes and Opacities are different for each of these examples, but the way that I worked was very similar. The focus for the working process is always experimenting, improvising, being open to changing my mind, and perhaps discovering something surprising along the way.

### Changing the Character of a Photo

For a commission of a 6' 8" tall, four-panel folding screen, the client and I explored a wide range of possible imagery, but eventually we settled on one of her family's favorite travel locations, a lake in Austria, as the subject. I scanned in her two snapshots taken with a panoramic camera, patching and compositing them together to form an image the correct proportion for the screen (Figure 3.27). (See Chapters 1 and 2 for

**3.27** My client's snapshots from a vacation on an Austrian lake, and a composited version of the snapshots sized to fit the proportions of the proposed folding screen.

examples of compositing and patching. See Chapter 9, "Simulating Installations of Your Work," for a mock-up of the final screen.)

Because I was going to interpret this image as a painting (with real paints), I wanted more than just a composited snapshot to work from. To help me create a painterly version that I could use as a source image, I altered the composited snapshot so it looked less like a photo. In creating duplicates of the original, I set different Blending modes and Opacities, and on the first duplicate, I even applied a filter effect. I chose Filter> Gaussian Blur and adjusted the setting until the image smoothed but was still visible (Figure 3.28).

**3.28** Applying a Gaussian Blur filter to a duplicate of the background photo layer.

I applied a Hue/Saturation Adjustment Layer (from the Adjustment Layers icon in the Layers palette) to make the image slightly richer and greener. After duplicating the original, I then moved it above the blurred version. Trying each of the Blending modes, I chose Darken (Figure 3.29).

On yet another duplicate of the original layer, I applied various filters (undoing when I didn't like it) and settled on Filter> Sketch> Bas Relief (Figure 3.30).

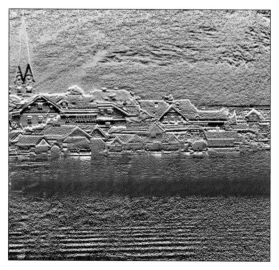

**3.29** After applying a Hue/Saturation Adjustment Layer, and a blurred duplicate of the original layer set to Darken Blending mode.

**3.30** Bas Relief filter applied to a duplicate of the original.

For the final version, I reduced the Opacity of the Bas Relief layer to 16% and applied a Levels Adjustment Layer to intensify the contrast. I brought a print of this version into my studio to use as a source for the large painting (Figure 3.31).

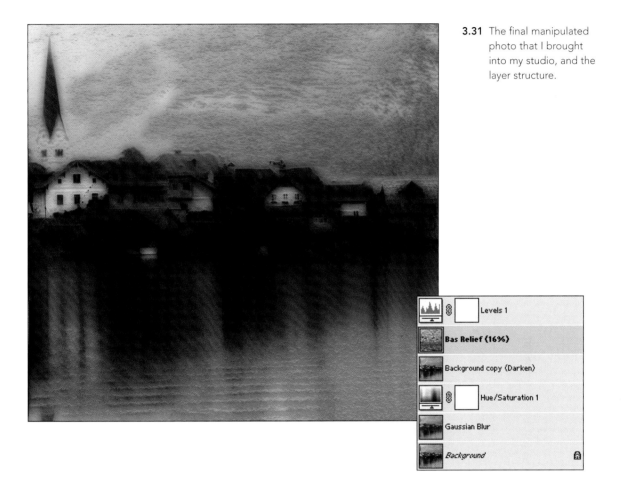

**3.31** The final manipulated photo that I brought into my studio, and the layer structure.

## Enhancing Simple Subjects

This process of duplicating layers and experimenting with Blending modes can come in handy when you need to enhance a boring image. I needed to quickly pull together a simulated thematic mural installation for a school gymnasium. I collected a series of sports balls in low resolution through the Internet. I first placed all the balls into one larger file using the Move tool and then repositioned them within their own layers to form the basic composition (Figure 3.32).

**3.32** All the balls in position in one large file.

I then renamed each of the layers and created a Layer Set to contain all of the balls. To create a Layer Set (something like a folder), click the first layer you want in the set to activate it, then link all the other layers you want to place in the set by clicking in the column next to the Eye icon to display its Link icon. With all of the layers that you want to place in the set linked, choose New Set From Linked from the Layers pop-up menu. With the balls all contained within a set, I created background layers for color behind the balls with dividing lines between them (Figure 3.33).

To transform these simple balls into something a bit more interesting, I first merged the Layer Set into one flattened layer. To merge a Layer Set, first select it in the Layers palette, and then choose Merge Layer Set from the Layers pop-up menu. To create a stylized effect, I duplicated the merged layer containing the balls twice, setting the first duplicate to Soft Light and the second to Hard Light (Figure 3.34).

**3.33** Low resolution sports balls collected in one document and placed into a Layer Set. The multi-colored background and dividing lines are on layers below, outside of the set.

**3.34** After duplicating the flattened balls and setting one duplicate to Soft Light and the other to Hard Light.

After adding finishing touches to the lines and adding a blurred shadow underneath, the balls were ready to be placed into the gymnasium as shown in Figure 3.35 (for more about this installation process, see Chapter 9).

**3.35** The final version of the balls, and then shown in a simulated installation as a mural on a gymnasium wall.

## More Exploration Suggestions

See if you can paint in corrections to a black and white image using layers above it set to Multiply (to darken) and Screen (to lighten).

On a color snapshot, try duplicating the image and experimenting with setting various Blending modes and Opacities to the duplicate.

Try transforming a black and white image into color by changing it to RGB color mode. Then create a new layer above the original image to contain the color, change it to Multiply mode, and paint into it with colors. Continue to experiment with changing the Blending mode and Opacity, duplicating layers, and repeating Blending mode and Opacity experimentation.

Try applying Blending modes without duplicating layers (thus keeping your file size much smaller)! Create a new Adjustment layer (choose any Adjustment Layer mode from the Adjustment Layer icon at the bottom of the Layers palette) but apply no adjustment and click OK. Experiment with changing the Blending mode to this Adjustment Layer.*

*This exploration suggestion evolved from a discovery by Katrin Eismann.

# CHAPTER 4

# Radical Ways to Generate New Ideas from Older, or "Finished" Work

Have you ever been stuck creatively and not known what to do next? If you really don't know in what direction to go creatively, let the computer kick-start your creative engine. Computers are great at randomly generating all sorts of things, and Photoshop provides many different ways to access this potential. All you really have to do is show Photoshop where to start, choose a direction, and then tell it when to stop. You can start with a blank screen and explore which effects will introduce enough visual material to respond to, or you can start off your process with any image you want. Once your creative engine is rolling again, you can harness all of the tools at your disposal to combine, composite, mask, or simplify any or all of your new images or variations.

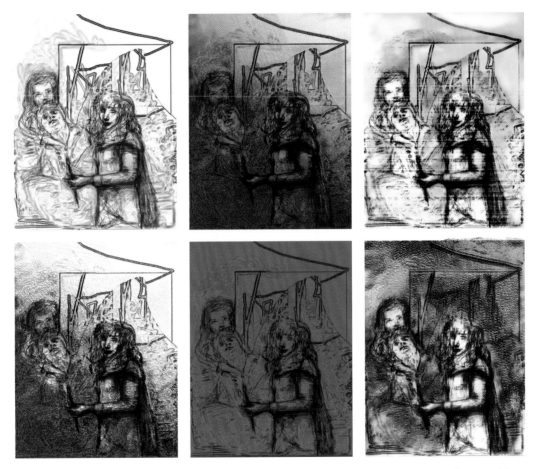

For "The Artist (grid)" I created new versions of an older image by applying various filters and effects, and then recombining the different versions.

Be sure to keep a log of what settings you use as you go along. Often you'll discover something that doesn't really work where you first applied it, but will eventually be perfect for something, sometime. Most of Photoshop filter and effect settings can be saved as you work, so if you find something you think you like, save the setting. Many of the effects maintain your last applied settings until you quit the program, so even after you've applied an effect, you can often reopen the effect and then save the settings.

To speed up your workflow, get in the habit of duplicating the layers that you're about to work with and apply your experimental effects to the duplicates. If the image that you want to work with exists on multiple layers, you'll have to make a merged copy of the visible layers (Edit> Copy Merged) and then paste to put the copy into its own layer. Before you apply an effect to this layer, rename it meaningfully, duplicate it, and then apply the effect to the duplicate.

In addition to applying filters and effects to duplicate layers, you can experiment with creating Adjustment Layers. Even though most people think of Adjustment Layers as a way to subtly correct problems in an image, you also can use Adjustment Layers to apply radical effects. And the beauty of Adjustment Layers is that they are saved within your layered file in an editable state, which can be applied to another image.

This is your opportunity to get completely lost in Photoshop. There are so many variables that you'll probably run out of time before you run out of things to try. So play, experiment, and have fun. Move through menu by menu, but start first with the Filter menu and Adjustment Layers. What you end up doing with your experiments is completely up to you. You might want to keep a book of printouts of different effects and how you achieved them so that the next time you're looking for inspiration, you can simply thumb through your printed results. However, you want to stay organized, make certain to do so well enough that you'll be able to replicate any effect you fall in love with.

## Radically Transforming an Image

With the aid of the computer, you can take an image and beat the heck out of it until you've transformed it into something completely different.

Just open your image, save a copy, and start applying filters and effects. Many of the effects work only in RGB mode, so if your image is grayscale or CMYK color space, then you'll need to first choose Image> Mode> RGB and then save this version of your image with a new name and in Photoshop format. If in applying filter upon filter you get too tangled up, you can Undo, or open the History Palette and locate a previous state. If all else fails, Revert to Saved and start over again. You can make your process a bit smoother by duplicating your image layer before you begin working on it (drag the layer to the New Layer icon) and then apply your effects to that duplicate layer. If you find something you like—before you do something else radical—duplicate your current layer and apply new effects to your new duplicate. In this way, you'll easily be able to delete your current layer and return quickly to the last stage that you were pleased with.

You don't have to be willing to deform one of your images to explore this chapter. Instead of transforming an existing image, a colleague of mine likes to start with a blank document, and then she looks for filters and effects that introduce enough information to work with—and then explores from there. If you want to try doing this, I suggest you start by exploring the Render and Texture sets of filters.

Transforming images one into another can become addictive. Whenever you're lucky enough to have time to be creative without a project waiting for you in the wings, simply begin with any image in Photoshop and distort and transform it until it becomes something else.

I began this first project with an image I called "The Museum." I wasn't thoroughly pleased with it but wanted to go in a different direction entirely. Not knowing where to go with it, my first try at an effect was Filter> Brush Strokes> Angled Strokes (Figure 4.1). This was still too close to the original image, so next I decided to try something more dramatic.

The Wave filter cannot only drastically alter your image, but if you're in the right mood it can provide you with hours of entertainment. Changing the number of fenerators and type of wave can create completely different, unexpected results. Adjusting the other parameters can allow you to fine-tune the effect. And if you really want to get somewhere unexpected, try clicking the Randomize option. Each time you Randomize, the wave will randomize. Given how radically this filter can alter your image, my choice was rather tame (Figure 4.2).

**4.1** To begin the transformation of an image, I applied the Angled Strokes filter.

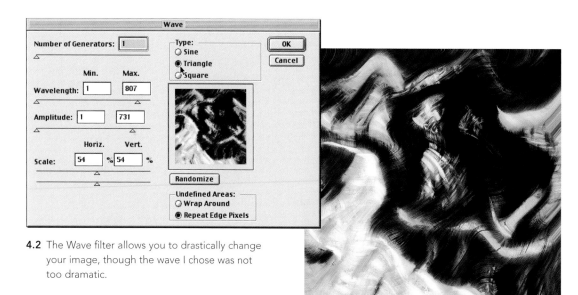

**4.2** The Wave filter allows you to drastically change your image, though the wave I chose was not too dramatic.

If before you apply the next effect, you duplicate the layer that contained the last effect and then apply the effect to the new duplicate, you'll be working in what I call *progressively stacked layers*. If you keep your previous version on a layer below, it is easy to return to your last stage while also giving you a permanent record of your progress. At any time you also can combine your latest altered version with the previous one by simply adjusting the Blending mode and or Opacity in the Layers palette.

After duplicating my Wave layer by dragging it over the New Layer icon, I transformed the duplicate and combined it back with the original wave using the Layers palette. To do this, I selected the duplicate layer by command-clicking it in the Layers palette (CTRL+click in Windows), I then chose Edit> Transform> Rotate 90°CCW (counter clockwise), and then Edit> Transform> Flip Vertical. The next step was to change the duplicate layer to the Screen Blending mode and adjust the Opacity to 60%, which blended the lights from the flipped and rotated version, with the original wave layer underneath (Figure 4.3). It was getting somewhere, but it was a bit too symmetrical.

**4.3** Duplicating the Wave Effect layer, I rotated and flipped the duplicated, then set the duplicate layer to Screen Blending mode with a 60% Opacity.

One of the many Distort filters with hidden power is the Shear filter. When you enter the filter (Filter> Distort> Shear), you'll see a grid containing a simple line with an editable point on either end. As you might guess, you can slide those endpoints within the grid to affect the shear. However, you might not know that by clicking anywhere else within the grid or on the line would place new points to the line, creating curves. Clicking and dragging on those points will adjust the curves (Figure 4.4). This will allow you to create asymmetrical effects. See how the Wrap Around and Repeat Edge Pixels change your image. Reset all the curves to the original line by clicking Default (or holding Option(Alt) and clicking the Reset button).

At any point you also can select a portion of your image and copy and paste your selection into its own layer. After you have a selection of your image isolated on its own layer, you can transform it and recombine it with the layers below using Blending mode and Opacity changes. You can apply new filters to this layer or use one of the simple Transform effects from the Edit menu. I selected an area of my image, copied and pasted the selection, then used the Edit> Transform command to rotate, skew, and scale the selection. When I applied it (by pressing Return), I set the layer to 40% Opacity (Figure 4.5).

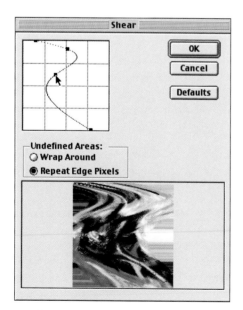

**4.4** Customizing the Shear tool to create an asymmetrical effect.

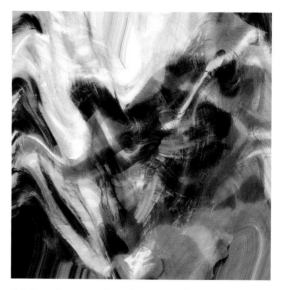

**4.5** Transforming selected portions of my image and combining it with the layers below by adjusting the Opacity.

With a section of the image overlaid on itself, I finally began to see something else to pursue as a composition. I saw the suggestions of figures, and using the painting tools and the Eyedropper tool to pick up colors from the image itself, I started drawing in the figures I saw.

To finish the image, "Figures," I chose a Curves adjustment (from the Adjustment Layer icon in the Layers palette) to make the image a bit more rosy and red (Figure 4.6).

**4.6** After I saw the suggestions of figures, I drew them in and at the end applied a "rosy" Curves adjustment to finalize "Figures."

## Reinterpreting an Existing Image

Try digging around for an old image to reinterpret. If the image isn't already digitized, then scan it into Photoshop. Save the image in Photoshop format (with a new name) and then duplicate the layer with the original image. You'll work into the duplicate, and then when you're ready to do something different, create another duplicate of the original layer and work on that duplicate. Save frequently and keep notes about what you're doing. To save a flat copy of the layers that are currently visible, use File> Save As, then choose TIFF format. Make certain to give these flat copies meaningful names so that you'll be able to identify them at a later time.

In 1990, in a program called ColorStudio, I created an image of an artist and her subjects. Saving the first version, I reworked "The Artist" into a second version, "The Artist II." (See Figure 4.7.) A decade later, I wanted

**4.7** "The Artist" and "The Artist II" were images I created in 1990 and wanted to rework in Photoshop.

**4.8** I applied Lighting Effects to the first duplicate, choosing Green for the Texture Channel.

to rework the image using Photoshop and the new ways of working I'd discovered in the intervening years.

Even the most obvious effects can produce unexpected results. After saving my first version of "The Artist" as a Photoshop document, I duplicated the layer containing the original image. The first effect I tried was a variant of the Lighting Effects filter. After choosing Filter> Render> Lighting Effects, I tried different effects. With Parallel Directional from the Style pop-up, I turned off the light by unchecking the On checkbox. For the Texture Channel, I selected Green and clicked OK (Figure 4.8).

Duplicating the original layer again, I applied the Filter> Noise> Add Noise filter to the next duplicate. By increasing the amount to 75%, the image became a field of texture. To the next duplicate, I applied the Grain filter (Filter> Texture> Grain) and chose the Horizontal option (Figure 4.9).

Some filters have a wide range of effects, which vary greatly with the settings. I applied the High Pass filter (Filter> Other> High Pass) to two different layers. To the first duplicate I applied a low Radius (3) and to the second duplicate I applied a higher setting (50), as shown in Figure 4.10.

**4.9** Working on duplicates of the original, I applied the Add Noise filter at 75% to one and the Grain filter with the Horizontal option to another.

**4.10** To two duplicate layers I applied the High Pass filter, one with a Radius of 3, another with a Radius of 50.

Experiment with all of the different Adjustment Layer options. Levels and Curves can do much more than just subtly color-correct an image; even these options allow you to move in radical directions. Choose the Pencil tool within Curves and just start scribbling (Figure 4.11). You'll find that fluid curves produce more subtle effects and staccato horizontal lines create more "posterized" effects. If your curves angle in the opposite direction from the default, you'll be inverting those colors. Try scribbling into the individual channels, as well as the overall RGB option.

**4.11** A version of the image after applying a radical Curves adjustment.

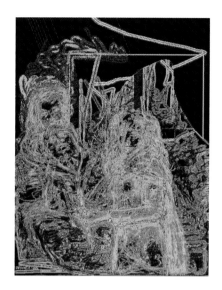

For some edgy effects, try Adjustment Layer> Gradient Map. It is probably meant for creating lovely gradients in mostly blank canvases, but it can wreak havoc on your image in the most surprising ways. After you choose Gradient Map, you'll be looking at a very conservative dialog box (Figure 4.12). You can choose additional gradient sets from the pop-up arrow and then append those sets to your current set, or you can replace the current set with the new selection.

Click the Gradient Map itself, and you get to a much more diverse set of options (Figure 4.13). Play a bit with all of the settings, but the key to opening a whole new world of options is to change the Gradient Type from Solid to Noise. With Noise chosen, your main variables are Roughness (a slider from 1 to 100%) and the wild and crazy Randomize. If at first you don't like, click again—just don't get carried away with clicking too fast because once you pass by a setting, you'll not get it again! If you think you like something, save it! Then go ahead and play some more.

**4.12** The first dialog box you encounter when you choose a Gradient Map Adjustment Layer.

**Gradient Map**

**Gradient Used for Grayscale Mapping**

OK

Cancel

☑ Preview

**Gradient Options**
☐ Dither
☐ Reverse

**4.13** After clicking the Gradient Map, you have a wealth of options to choose from. The second image is the final map I chose and the image with the map applied.

After I had accumulated a batch of separate TIFF files that were variations on my original image, I used the Move tool to drag them all (along with the original two versions) into one layered Photoshop file. (Hold the Shift key as you drag images into another file of the same dimensions to keep them aligned.) Then by using techniques described more fully in Chapter 5, "Nonlinear Creativity," I combined the various versions by attaching Layer Masks, changing Blending modes, and setting custom Opacities. Whenever I'd find a version I liked, I'd create a merged copy of the visible layers (Edit> Copy Merged), then create a New document (which is automatically sized to my copy), and then paste the merged copy into the new file. Saving the flat version of the file in TIFF format, I could use that version as a final or recombine it with others at any time. At the end of the process, there were four new versions that I liked (in addition to the two original ones). I made a large blank canvas and brought in all six variations of the image that I liked and used the Move tool to organize them into the final grid version of the image (Figure 4.14).

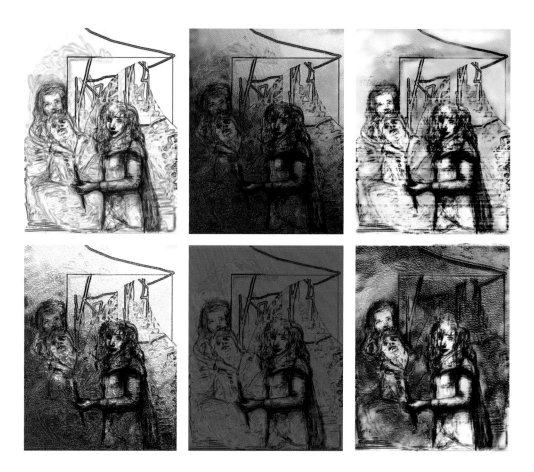

**4.14** The final image in which four new versions are united with the original to form a grid, and a portion of the Layers palette showing various versions being combined using Layers Masks.

## More Exploration Suggestions

Try creating multiple variations from one of the more complex filters or effects, such as the Distort> Wave filter or the Gradient Map Adjustment Layer.

- Begin with any image and transform it using filters and effects until you see another idea or image emerge. Use progressive layers to keep track of each phase of your transformations and develop your new image using painting tools or compositing techniques.

- From the Tool Preset Picker in the upper right of the toolbar, load New Presets for the Brush tool (see the Adobe Help documents for help loading and locating the brush Presets). Choose a brush that creates vibrant, multi-textured, multi-colored marks and start covering your blank canvas, or a blank layer above an existing image. Keep making marks until you are inspired to go in a new direction. Place different images below the brush marks to see how they interact with your painting.

- Try beginning with a blank new file and use the Render and Texture filters to introduce enough visual material to your image to work with, and then transform this material into something else.*

- Create variations on an image using filters and effects and then recombine the variations using Layer Masks and Blending modes (see Chapter 3, "Improvising with Color Using Layers," for detailed suggestions about this way of working).

*This exploration suggestion contributed by Sandee Cohen.

# CHAPTER 5

# Nonlinear Creativity

Like our lives, our traditional art unfolds and develops in linear directions. We are constantly forced to choose to follow one path or another. Do you keep an image as it is or risk what you currently have to explore where that creative direction will lead?

Nonlinear creativity is a completely different way of thinking. By applying nonlinear logic, you can more fully take advantage of the uniqueness of the computer as a creative medium and perhaps even invite your computer to participate in your creative process.

Photoshop provides us with many ways in which to pursue nonlinear creativity. You can keep something as it is (by saving) and then also continue to develop the image. Photoshop can support you in taking great artistic risks; as long as you consistently save your work in stages, you're actually not risking anything at all.

Six of the dozens of images that were created by combining a few source images using Blending mode and Opacity changes.

But the concept of nonlinear creativity can be taken much further than just knowing that you can return to a saved version of an image. You can pursue multiple paths from one saved stage. You can use Layer Masks to combine a portion of an earlier version with a later one. You can recover any earlier saved phase to follow an entirely new creative direction. You can even combine multiple versions of one image, or a number of similar images, in ways that are certain to surprise you.

Nonlinear thinking can both enhance your familiar working processes and introduce you to entirely new approaches to creating art. With an open mind you can explore new ways of thinking and expand your work in creative directions that would once have seemed impossible within the confines of our traditional, linear lives.

## Recovering Lost Stages

In traditional printmaking, you develop an image onto a plate in reverse. To see the results of what you've done to the plate so far, you pull a proof (print the plate). These intermediary proofs are called *states*. At any time you can decide that this current state is the final version, and then you can pull an edition of that image, which requires that you determine how many prints there will ever be of that final state of your plate. When you decide to continue developing an image, except for the proofs that you've already printed, the intermediate states are forever limited to the prints that you proofed along the way.

When working on the computer, if you save incrementally as you work, you can actually return to and recover a previous state of an image. As you work on your images, make notes about saved stages that particularly intrigue you. At any time you can return to that saved version to explore variations or move in completely different directions.

With your start safely saved, you can try anything and work with any tool. Whenever you get something you like, choose Save As and give the file a new meaningful name. Try and keep a journal to record the names of files to which you'd like to return.

For this project, I used painting tools to draw over an amorphous image, saving the stages incrementally as I worked. The first two stages of scribbles on top of the initial image proved to be fertile starting points for a number of different directions (Figure 5.1).

As long as you remember to save any versions you think have potential as you work, you can continue to freely experiment with painting tools. At this stage I saw many different possibilities, so I noted the names of the files and then continued working. At first I worked on further defining the emerging figures I call "Cave Figures" using painting tools and then used Levels (from the Adjustment Layer icon in the Layers palette) to change the color cast of the image (Figure 5.2).

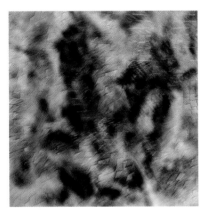 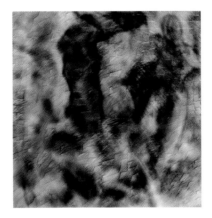

**5.1** The first two stages of scribbles on top of the starting image proved to be starting points to which I kept returning.

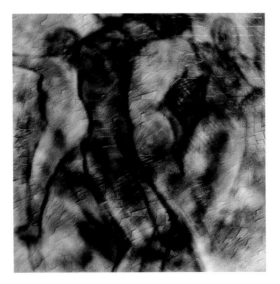

**5.2** The first direction that I followed from the start image.

After you've followed one path, try starting again from the same beginning image and see if there's another direction that you can follow. Returning to the second scribble stage of the original start, I used painting tools and began to sketch over the shapes that implied a bearded figure on the left and then the figure on the right (Figure 5.3).

Then using Levels and Curves (from the Adjustment Layer pop-up in the Layers palette), I changed the color cast of the image. Using Filter> Brush Strokes> Accented Edges, I experimented until I got an effect I liked (Figure 5.4).

**5.3** Starting again from the second scribble stage, I drew in the bearded figure.

**5.4** Changing the color cast and applying the Brush Strokes filter.

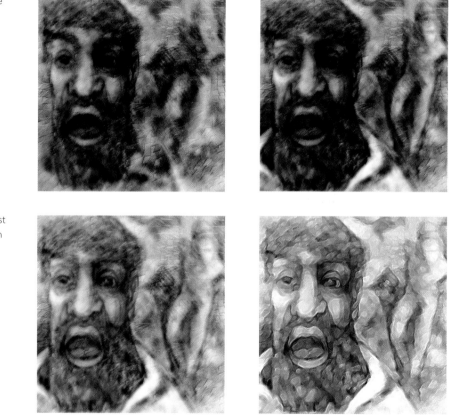

Noting the figure on the right as something that I would (someday) return to, I selected the head, chose Image> Crop, and saved this version. I then applied Filter> Distort> Twirl to change the expression of the face and saved a number of different versions. Though I was intending to choose a version, while I was viewing the images side by side, I decided to combine them into the final "Three Faces" (Figure 5.5).

**5.5** Cropping the face, I applied the Twirl filter a number of different ways and then combined three to form the final triptych, "Three Faces."

Returning this time to the first scribble stage, I hoped to find a completely different inspiration to follow. I started by flipping the image (Image> Rotate> Flip Horizontal). Then to change the palette, I inverted the colors (choose Invert from the Adjustment Layers icon in the Layers palette) and then chose Curves (also from the Adjustment Layers icon) for some further color adjustments. I was still distracted by the shapes that had originally led to the "Cave Figures," so I next rotated the canvas clockwise (Image> Rotate> 90°CW).

With the image flipped and rotated in the new palette, I finally saw a new direction to move in. Drawing next with the painting tools, I traced the edges, finding bones and sculls (Figure 5.6). For the final version of "Bones," I continued to paint in details and then darkened the image using Levels (from the Adjustment Layers icon).

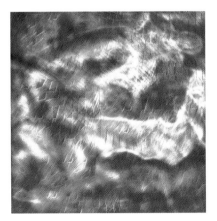

**5.6** Returning to the first scribble stage, I changed the perspective of the image by flipping it, inverting and adjusting the colors, and then rotating it.

91

Though the final images, "Cave Figures," "Three Faces," and "Bones," look nothing alike, they all evolved from the same starting image—something impossible to achieve working with traditional media (Figure 5.7).

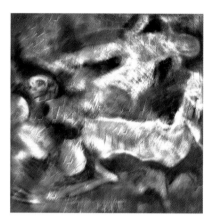

**5.7** Sketching in the bones and skulls, and the final "Bones" image.

## Combining Multiple Versions or Similar Images

Using Photoshop, you can combine multiple versions of an image, regardless of the medium in which they were created. Chapter 3, "Improvising with Color Using Layers," demonstrates different ways to stack versions of the same image on top of itself, changing the Blending mode and Opacity. To add a nonlinear twist to this process, this project combines different but related images on top of each other while adjusting Blending modes and Opacity.

See if you have a series of similar images with which you'd like to experiment. I had a series of monotypes that I'd created using the same snapshot as a template (see Chapter 7, "Creating Monotypes from Digital Images," for how I created these monotypes). I wanted to see what would happen if I combined the various monotypes with the original snapshot of the Etruscan figures (Figure 5.8).

**5.8** The badly exposed snapshot of Etruscan figures, and two of the monotypes that I created using the snapshot as a template.

To create a digital interpretation of this Etruscan imagery, I wanted to combine the various versions on top of each other in alignment. Though you could combine images without aligning them, I started by making sure that each of the images was the same size and was lined up properly. The images of the monotypes were 6″ squares, and the scanned snapshot was rectangular—all of the images were off-center with uneven borders.

To create the version, to which all others would be aligned, I started by showing the rulers (Command+R for Mac, Ctrl+R for Windows) and then created guidelines to align with the image. To make the guidelines, with your rulers showing, click and hold within the ruler area and drag into the image to pull out a guide. Let go of the mouse or stylus button when the guide is in the correct location. To enlarge the canvas to form a uniform border around the image, I used Image> Canvas Size. In Canvas

Size, use the iconic thumbnails to locate the placement of the current image in relation to where the new canvas would be added, increase the dimensions as needed, and click OK. After the monotype was centered, I used patching and color correction techniques (as described in the Chapter 2, "Creative Problem Solving Using Layers") to clean up the border around the monotype (Figure 5.9).

If you want to align images before combining them, you'll need to first prepare them all so they match in size and proportion. I used the Move tool to first bring the scan of the black monotype into the file with the guidelines and then move it into position using the guides. I then continued to use patching techniques to fill out the border and clean up the scan.

I also brought the scanned snapshot into the document with the guidelines so I could combine it with the monotypes. I used patching techniques to stretch and copy portions of the snapshot image to match the 6" square dimensions of the monotypes (Figure 5.10).

After combining different images into one file, you can use the Layers palette to hide and reveal layers to show the different versions.

**5.9** Creating guidelines for the monotype and then using patching techniques to create a uniform border around it.

**5.10** The scanned snapshot using patching techniques to match the 6" square dimensions of the monotypes.

After aligning your images, start to experiment with different ways of combining them by changing the Blending modes and Opacities. I began with two of the monotypes in one file with a white bottom layer (Figure 5.11). With the Peach monotype on top of the Blue one, I set the Peach layer to Multiply Blending mode. It already seemed too dark, so I reduced the Opacity of the Blue layer, stopping at 54% (Figure 5.12).

**5.11** The first two monotypes that I placed into one file so that I could combine them.

**5.12** Setting the top Peach monotype layer to Multiply mode, reducing the Opacity to 54%, and the Layers palette.

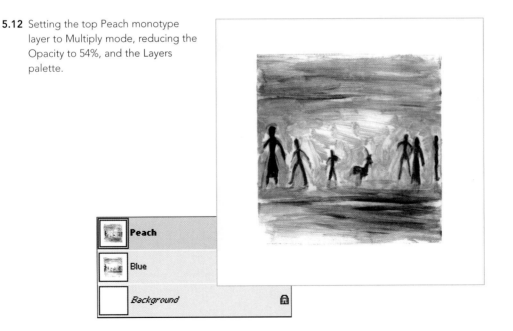

Try duplicating a layer by dragging it over the New Layer icon in the Layers palette. Once duplicated, you can again experiment with changing the Blending mode and Opacity of various layers. I first made a duplicate of the Blue layer and selected each of the modes, one at a time, until I settled on Soft Light (Figure 5.13). It can be helpful to rename your layers as you go.

Perhaps there are more images that you'd like to incorporate into in your composition. I wanted to combine the monotypes with the squared-off version of the original snapshot. Trying different Blending modes for the snapshot, I chose Hard Light. I duplicated the snapshot layer and then duplicated it again and again until there were four snapshot layers, all set to Hard Light (Figure 5.14).

**5.13** The Layers palette after duplicating the Blue layer and renaming the layers.

**5.14** Bringing the snapshot into the layered file, then after duplicating the snapshot three times, and the Layers palette with the four snapshot layers.

Continue to experiment with duplicating layers. This time move the duplicates around in the layers order first, then change the Blending mode. To move a layer in the Layers palette, just grab it and drag it to the new location. I duplicated the Blue monotype 54% layer again and this time moved the duplicate above the snapshot layers. Experimenting with Blending modes, I found a quite different effect with Exclusion (Figure 5.15).

If you find something you like, use Save As to save a flat copy of your currently visible layers. I use Save As and then choose TIFF format to save the flat version, giving it a meaningful name so that I can reconstruct how I created it more easily. Also periodically use Save As to save incremental versions of your layered file in Photoshop format. After you have what you like saved to disk, see if you can create variations of that version. I liked what Exclusion did with the Blue monotype, so I next duplicated the Peach monotype, moved it to the top of the layer order, and set this Peach layer to Exclusion as well (Figure 5.16). I then properly renamed the Exclusion duplicates.

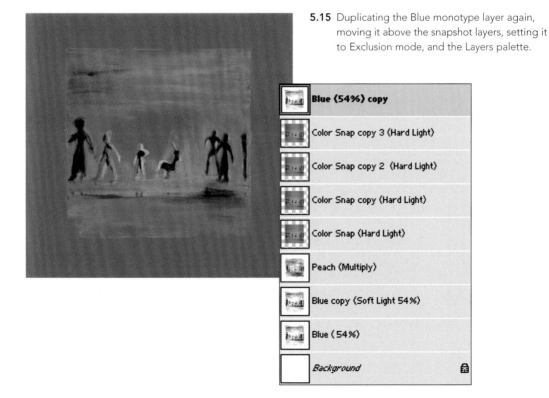

**5.15** Duplicating the Blue monotype layer again, moving it above the snapshot layers, setting it to Exclusion mode, and the Layers palette.

Blue (54%) copy

Color Snap copy 3 (Hard Light)

Color Snap copy 2 (Hard Light)

Color Snap copy (Hard Light)

Color Snap (Hard Light)

Peach (Multiply)

Blue copy (Soft Light 54%)

Blue (54%)

*Background*

For further experimentation, revisit the Opacities that you set earlier in the procedure and then try hiding and showing different layers. I changed the topmost Blue layer to 100% Opacity, which created an ivory-toned version.

Finally, with the Blue layer still set to 100% Opacity, completely hiding the top Peach layer created an entirely different result (Figure 5.17).

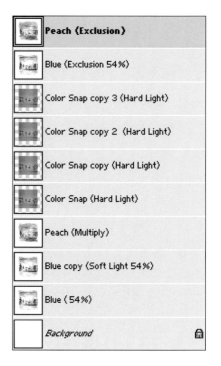

**5.16** Duplicating the Peach layer, moving it above and setting it to Exclusion mode, and the Layers palette.

**5.17** With the Blue layer still set to 100% Opacity, the result of hiding the top Peach layer.

## Stacking and Masking Variations

You can expand the possibilities of any effect by integrating nonlinear thinking. In this case, the nonlinear thinking that I've employed is that the computer magically allows you combine different versions of the same image to create a new whole. This project uses a variant on the photographic-to-painterly effect in Chapter 3 but then expands nonlinearly by continuing to reintroduce and recombine variations of the image with itself.

After compositing dozens of digital photos to create an imaginary interior (see Chapter 6, "Compositional Brainstorming," for how this image was constructed), I wanted to begin my experiments by recreating part of the painterly effect I'd discovered when creating another image (Figure 5.18).

**5.18** An imaginary interior composited from dozens of digital photos.

To create your own version of this painterly effect, duplicate your original Background image (drag the Background layer over the New Layer icon in the Layers palette). To this duplicate, apply a filter that simplifies the shapes and write down the name of the filter and specific settings that you choose. In Chapter 3, I used the Gaussian Blur filter, and for the

"Interior" image, I applied the Dust & Scratches filter instead (Filter> Noise> Dust & Scratches). For this relatively low-resolution image, the settings I used were a Radius of 5 and a Threshold of 24. After you've simplified the shapes in the first duplicate, duplicate the Background layer again and this time drag the duplicate above the simplified layer in the Layers palette. Set this new background duplicate to Darken Blending mode (Figure 5.19).

**5.19** After applying the Dust & Scratches filter to the first duplicate of the Background, then moving the second duplicate to the top and setting it to Darken Blending mode, and the Layers palette.

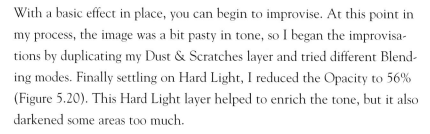

With a basic effect in place, you can begin to improvise. At this point in my process, the image was a bit pasty in tone, so I began the improvisations by duplicating my Dust & Scratches layer and tried different Blending modes. Finally settling on Hard Light, I reduced the Opacity to 56% (Figure 5.20). This Hard Light layer helped to enrich the tone, but it also darkened some areas too much.

If you like what a layer does to part of the image but not to other areas, create a Layer Mask. To add a Layer Mask to the current layer, click the Layer Mask icon in the Layers palette. After you've added a Layer Mask, you'll see a new thumbnail representing the Mask in the Layers palette, as well as the new Layer Mask icon next to the Eye icon, which indicates that your layer's mask is active (targeted). To work on a layer click its thumbnail, and to work on a Layer Mask target the mask thumbnail. By default, a blank Layer Mask is white, which allows the entire layer to initially be visible.

**5.20** After duplicating the Dust & Scratches layer and changing the duplicate to Hard Light Blending mode and then reducing the Opacity to 56%.

To mask areas of the current layer so it's not visible, paint with black into the Layer Mask using the painting tools. Use white to restore the mask to transparent. If you paint with grays you'll be creating a semi-transparent mask, allowing the image above to blend with the image below. You also can use selection tools to define an area and then fill the selection with black, white, grays, or gradients. I painted with black and grays into the Hard Light Layer Mask to reduce its effect in specific areas where I wanted to see more detail (especially around the figure and the vase).

At any point in your process, you can make a flat copy of your currently visible layers and then combine that copy with the layers below using Blending modes. To make a copy of your currently visible layers, choose Edit> Select All (Command+A for Mac or Ctrl+A for Windows) and then Edit> Copy Merged (Command+Shift+C for Mac or Ctrl+Shift+C for Windows). For Copy Merged to be available, you'll have to make sure that your current layer is visible (if it doesn't work, in your Layers palette, click one of the visible layers). To place this merged copy into a new layer directly above your current layer, just Edit> Paste (Command+V for Mac or Ctrl+V for Windows). After the merged copy is on its own layer, you can experiment with changing the Blending mode so it can combine with the layers below. I chose Hard Light Blending mode for my first merged copy and then reduced the Opacity to 63%.

If you find a Blending mode you like, you might want to paste in the merged copy again. With the copy still on the Clipboard, I pasted the copy into a new layer. I decided on Soft Light Blending mode for this second merged copy (Figure 5.21).

**5.21** Pasting another copy of the image on the Clipboard and then setting this copy to Soft Light Blending mode.

Applying some Blending modes can over-saturate and darken an image too much. Use Adjustment Layers to lighten, darken, change hues, contrast, or saturate. I wanted to reduce the saturation of most of the colors in the image, so I chose Hue/Saturation from the Adjustment Layers icon in the Layers palette. I reduced the Saturation overall and clicked OK. In later versions of Photoshop, Adjustment Layers have Layer Masks automatically attached; to bring back some of the saturation selectively in a few spots, I painted with black into this Layer Mask. (If your version of Photoshop doesn't have a Layer Mask attached, create one for the selected layer by clicking the Layer Mask icon.)

You don't have to achieve all changes in one adjustment; I created a separate Levels Adjustment Layer to lighten the entire image just a bit (Figure 5.22).

At this point in the process, I needed to revise the original Background image that had become the basis for all the effect modifications. Returning to the original many-layered file that was the source for the composition, I rotated the rug so it aligned with the room, added more detail to the desk area, moved the table slightly, and changed the view through the glass door. After the original image was corrected and final in terms of composition, I had to reapply the painterly effect to this new image (Figure 5.23).

**5.22** The image and Layers palette with two Adjustment Layers applied.

**5.23** Going back to the original source image that was the basis for the effects file, I updated the composition.

Just because your working method is improvisational doesn't mean that an achieved effect is unrepeatable. By following a few methodical steps you should be able to update the composition while maintaining your effect. Before you begin updating your image, make certain that all of your layers are meaningfully named to include the Blending mode and Opacity settings. Double-click a layer to rename it (depending on your version of Photoshop, you might need to hold Option for Mac or Alt for Windows to rename a layer). Make sure you also use Save As to save a new version of your current layered file so that you can return to it later if you mess up.

The next steps might vary a bit if your effects document is constructed differently from mine, but the principles are the same. You'll be replacing each of the old effect layers with your new image, one layer at a time. So that you can follow along if you want, I'll assume that you are working with the same painterly effect that I described earlier.

With your effects document ready, open the new source image, select all, and copy (or Copy Merged if it's a layered image). Returning to your effects layered file, click the current Background layer and paste the new version. The new version should now be in a layer directly above the Background, so next hold down Command+E (for Mac) or Ctrl+D (for Windows) to Merge Down (Layer menu) and replace the old Background with the new image (Figure 5.24).

With your Background now containing your new image, duplicate the Background and move it above the next layer that you need to replace. If the layer you'll be replacing had an effect applied (such as Filter> Noise> Dust & Scratches), then look up the settings that you recorded and apply that filter to the new layer. If you forgot to record the settings but remember the filter, don't worry yet—there's a good chance that Photoshop remembered the settings for you. After you've applied the filters to the new layer, you're ready to Merge Down (Command+E or Ctrl+E), replacing the image on the old layer with the new one. If the layer that you're replacing had a Layer Mask, you'll get a dialog box asking if you want to Preserve the mask—click Preserve. If your original layer had an Opacity of less than 100%, then you'll need to reset your Opacity, but the layer should retain your layer name and Blending mode!

Repeat this process, duplicating the appropriate layer (such as Background or Dust & Scratches), moving it into position above the next layer that needs replacing, replicating any filters or effects, and pasting the new layer down on top of the old, while preserving any Layer Masks (and if necessary, resetting the Opacity).

Once the new image has replaced the previous one in all layers, feel free to continue to work and to apply finishing touches to the image. To make selective changes in the colors and the feeling of light, I began by painting into the Layer Mask for the Levels Adjustment Layer. To brighten up just a few more spots, I duplicated the Levels layer, reworked its Layer Mask, and repeated with a third Levels layer. Then I increased the Saturation in some spots by creating another Hue/Saturation Adjustment Layer and working into its mask.

Nonlinear also can mean reintroducing the original back into the version with effects applied, even at the last moment. The last thing I wanted to do to the image was to add back in some of the detail that was lost through the application of the effects. I duplicated the Background layer and moved it to the top position in the Layers palette. If you hold Option (Mac) or Alt (Windows) when you click the Layer Mask icon, instead of a white transparent mask, you'll create a completely opaque black Layer Mask. Now painting with white, you can selectively paint in the detail in the desired areas (Figure 5.25).

**5.25** The final image and its Layers palette.

Background copy

Hue/Saturation 2

Levels 1 copy 2

Levels 1 copy

Levels 1

Hue/Saturation 1

Merged Copy of below (SL 100%)

Merged Copy of below (HL 63%)

Background (darken)

Dust (hard light 56%)

Dust & Scratches 5/24

*Background*

## More Exploration Suggestions

Create a number of different images by returning again and again to the same start point and moving in different creative directions.

Place similar images in the same file with and without aligning them and experiment with various layers' Blending modes and Opacities.

In a multi-layered file, make merged copies of the visible layers (Edit> Copy Merged), paste the copy on top of the multi-layered file, and experiment with changing the Blending mode and Opacity of the merged copy.

Make variations of an image in one layered document and use Layer Masks to combine selective parts of the different layers.

In a multi-layered file, experiment with how the overall effects are altered by changing Blending modes and Opacity, hiding and showing layers, and changing the layer order.

CHAPTER 6

# Compositional Brainstorming

Regardless of what final form or medium your work eventually takes, the computer can provide you with a risk-free environment for working through compositional problems and exploring new directions. And because Photoshop allows you to explore different possible directions rather quickly, you can often speed up the creative process itself.

If you're a photographer, exploring compositional options could inspire you to composite or combine images or maybe even to reshoot taking into consideration what you've discovered through your explorations.

Now that I have begun to work through compositional problem-solving using Photoshop, whenever I'm stuck as to which direction to take with an oil painting, I'll bring the image into the computer and work on it there. After the problem has been resolved, I'll bring the print back into the studio, using the computer print as a source image.

A collection of snapshots and the imaginary place that I created from those (and other) snapshots.

An oil sketch, digitally working out the composition, and the final oil painting painted using the digital print (at left) as a source.

With some projects, using the computer might enable you to develop compositions not possible in other media. You can insert elements within a composition using layers. You can even create wholly (or partly) imaginary places by piecing together a series of photos or images. These places can become final works in themselves or can serve as source images for work in other media.

Knowing that you can easily insert elements into a composition, construct an imaginary place or brainstorm directions for work in other media that can help you to envision a broader range of creative possibilities for enhancing, reworking, and resolving images. Ultimately, the process of envisioning new possibilities and different ways of working does more than just help you to resolve the issue at hand—it expands your creative potential.

## Brainstorming New Directions

As long as you get your image into Photoshop, you can use Photoshop's tools to work through critical compositional decisions. Sometimes your digital works might become final artistic images in themselves. Other times, these digital images merely serve to guide the direction of the work in a different medium.

For almost two decades my digital art world remained completely separate from my traditional painting world. When I didn't know what to do with an unresolved oil painting I'd simply put it aside until I knew what to do or was fed up enough to paint over it and start a new painting on top of it. By digitizing work begun in any medium, I now use digital tools to work through creative stumbling blocks. Photoshop provides me with the tools and risk-free environment for accelerating the creative process of exploring what to do next.

### Changes in the Compositional Elements

The first oil painting that I brought into the computer to work on had languished in my painting studio for many years. It was just the bare bones of an oil sketch (see Figure 6.1). I knew that I wanted to do something with it, yet I was somehow sufficiently intimidated by it that I was incapable of doing anything further with it at all.

With the original oil sketch safe and intact, bringing the imagery into the computer enabled me to get past my inhibitions so I could finally begin to rework the image. Using painting tools, I freely painted on top of the image, saving incrementally as I went so I could always return to a previous stage. When I arrived at the image of the girl on the bed, I felt that I was ready to return to the actual painting. I printed out the image and brought the print into my painting studio (see Figure 6.2).

**6.1** The first oil sketch that I experimented with in Photoshop.

**6.2** Reworking the oil sketch in Photoshop until I reached a stage that I liked.

I love the challenge of painting and drawing by eye, but if you prefer, you can trace your computer image onto your canvas, paper, or board using a slide or overhead projector. To use a slide projector, you'll have to find a service bureau that can convert your digital images into transparency slides. If your local professional photo labs can't produce slides from your digital slides, all major cities have service bureaus that accept your disks by mail or via the Internet. To use an overhead projector, you'll need to print your image on transparency film (if your printer won't work with transparency film, many copy shops and service bureaus can copy your paper print onto transparent film for you).

After your transparency has been created, use the appropriate projector to project onto your canvas, board, or paper. If the projected image is too large, move the projector closer to the surface. If the image is too small, move the projector back. Then use any tools you want to trace the computer image onto your painting or drawing surface. To gauge your progress, periodically turn off the projector.

I taped my printed digital image to my easel so I could use the print as a reference, and began to paint over my oil sketch. After I had incorporated the elements from the digital image that I needed, I put aside the print and continued to work on the painting. Though the final painting, "The Attic Room," (see Figure 6.3) migrated somewhat from the digital version, without the help of the computer I might never have gotten up the nerve to work on the oil sketch—much less arrive at this imagery.

**6.3** A snapshot of the oil painting created using the digital print as a reference, and the final oil painting of "The Attic Room."

## Changes in Color and Lighting

You can use the computer to work out any issue you're struggling with, including exploring the different possible color and light directions that your work can take. Try experimenting with the Lighting Effects filter and applying different Adjustment Layers to change the color environment of your image.

With my "Monkey and the Turban" painting (see Figure 6.4), I had the compositional structure in place but wanted some inspiration as to where I should take the overall color and light.

**6.4** A digital snapshot of the original painting, which is in need of color direction.

Before you apply Lighting Effects to an image, it's a good idea to work on a duplicate, not the original. If your image is in multiple layers, you'll have to make a merged copy of the multi-layered image to apply the effect. Select All (Edit menu), Edit> Copy Merged, and then Paste to paste a flat copy of the visible layers into a new layer.

I started with a digital snapshot of my painting and then duplicated the Background layer by dragging it to the New Layer icon in the Layers palette. With this new duplicate layer active, I chose Filter> Render> Lighting Effects. I tried many of the default Lighting Effects and chose the

Crossing Style as my starting point. In the Preview of the effect I swung the direction of the light around, adjusted the size of the light, changed the colors for the Light Type and Ambient Light, and adjusted the Ambience setting (see Figure 6.5). I then saved the settings using the Save button under the Style button and clicked OK.

It was an interesting effect but didn't do enough for me, so I experimented with changing the Blending mode of the layer with the Lighting Effects applied. I liked the way the Saturation Blending mode interacted with the original image on the layer below, but I wasn't done yet. I next duplicated that layer and tried setting different Blending modes for that layer, settling on Hard Light at 51% Opacity (see Figure 6.6).

**6.5** Starting with one of the default Lighting Effects, I customized the effect, saved it, and applied it to the digital snapshot.

**6.6** Changing the Lighting Effects layer to Saturation Blending mode and then duplicating it and setting the duplicate layer to Hard Light at 50% Opacity.

I printed out the version of the digital snapshot with the Lighting Effects, brought the print into my painting studio, and continued to work on the painting.

Stay open to continuing opportunities to enlist the computer for help with decision-making. As my painting evolved, I reached a point where I once again needed to work through some color decisions in Photoshop.

This time I used a series of Adjustment Layers to change the colors in my digital snapshot. Choosing an Adjustment Layer from the Adjustment Layer icon in the Layers palette, I then fiddled with the adjustments until I got something I liked. To control how that adjustment was applied, I worked into the Layer Mask for that Adjustment Layer with black, white, and grays using the painting tools. Sometimes I'd duplicate the Adjustment Layer; sometimes I'd see what would happen if I changed the Blending mode or Opacity. Finally, with a number of Adjustment Layers stacked on top of each other, most with Layer Masks, I arrived at a version that gave me a new color direction for the painting (see Figure 6.7).

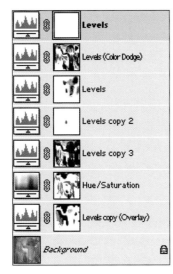

**6.7** Having evolved the painting to a stage where I needed more help with color decisions, I brought another digital snapshot into Photoshop and used a number of Adjustment Layers with Layer Masks to establish a new color direction.

115

With my new printout taped to my easel, I brightened up the greens and the golds in the painting and brought out some of the highlights. As the figures became more resolved, I put the printout away, finishing the painting on my own (see Figure 6.8).

**6.8** The final painting, "The Monkey and the Turban."

### Changes in Composition Elements, Color, and Lighting

Sometimes you might need to explore both color and compositional directions with the computer. "Three Angels" was another oil sketch that I was afraid to work on. I brought a digital snapshot of it into Photoshop, duplicated the layer with the image (dragging the layer to the New Layer icon), then chose Filter> Render> Lighting Effect, and applied an effect that lightened and brightened the image. I then duplicated that layer and applied another Lighting Effect to it, a wash of warm yellow light.

You can use Layer Masks to control how each of your effects layers will be applied. To do this for the original effect layer, I first hid the top, warm yellow layer. Next, I created a Layer Mask for the visible effect layer by clicking the Layer Mask icon. Using the painting tools, I painted into Layer Masks with black and grays to mask out where the effect would be applied and white to reapply it (see Figure 6.9).

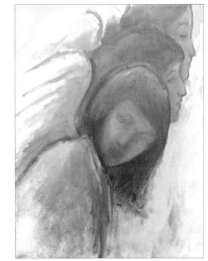

**6.9** The snapshot of the original oil sketch with the first lighting effect applied.

Showing the warm yellow layer, I held down the Option key when I created a Layer Mask for this layer (for Windows hold Alt) to create an opaque mask that entirely blocked the effect of the yellow light. I then used the painting tools to paint with white and grays where I wanted the yellow light to show through (black returns the mask to opaque) on the shoulder, the tops of the heads, and the wings.

You also can use the separate color channels of a Levels or Curves Adjustment Layer to affect the colors, values, and saturation of your image. Choose Levels or Curves from the Adjustment Layer icon in the Layers palette. Then from the Channel pop-up, select one of the separate channels and experiment with making adjustments. I chose each of the Red, Green, and Blue channels separately and made adjustments to each (see Figure 6.10).

To paint over your image, you'll want to create a new layer on top (click the New Layer icon). You can just begin painting, or you can set the Blending mode for this layer to change how the new layer will interact with the layers underneath. Experiment to see how each mode affects the marks you make within the layer—essentially Multiply Blending mode darkens your image, Screen lightens, and Overlay blends your colors with the image below using Screen for the lights and Multiply for the darks. I created a new layer, set it to Overlay Blending mode, and used the painting tools to add detail to the image (see Figure 6.11).

I brought the printout to my painting studio. This time, however, instead of referring loosely to the printout for ideas and suggestions, I actually used the printout as if it were a model and referred to it through the entire process of finishing the painting.

**6.10** The second lighting effect visible, then with a Layer Mask applied, and then after applying a Levels Adjustment Layer to darken the darks.

**6.11** With a new layer set to Overlay Blending mode, I painted in details, shown with the final layers structure of the digital version of "Three Angels," and then the final painted image created using the digital print as a reference.

## Creating an Imaginary Place

Traditionally, artists create sketches to quickly work through compositional ideas. Unfortunately, although *you* might be able to visualize how your sketch might be transformed into a finished image, clients are notoriously incapable of envisioning anything beyond what they see in front of them. When a client thought she wanted me to create an interior/exterior scene for a folding screen, I decided to try something new. Instead of beginning with sketches, I decided to piece together digital snapshots to create a composition that would both be easier for the client to interpret and could also eventually serve as a reference for me to use in creating the actual painted screen. Along the way, I discovered a method for creating imaginary places. So even though the folding screen project ended up going in an entirely different direction, I completely fell in love with this new way of working. (See Chapter 5, "Nonlinear Creativity," for the composition the client chose for the screen.)

If you don't have access to a digital camera, you can scan prints instead— it's just that using digital snapshots is so quick and immediate and saves bundles on processing fees. You can shoot shots and assemble later, or you can have a composition in mind and gather material for that vision. Because you move through ideas quickly with this way of working, I encourage you to be less careful and more spontaneous. Don't worry about creating perfect masks until you are relatively sure that this is the final version. Just relax and think of this as a loose sketching process.

I needed source material for creating the interior/exterior composition, and my mother's house was ideal. Her upstairs and downstairs have similar windows and doors, she had lovely decks, water views out the windows, and her furniture and design taste is exquisite. Grabbing my low-resolution digital snapshot camera, I went out for a visit.

I envisioned a scene with the interior at the left, with a glass door leading to the exterior deck to the right, and shot the snapshots accordingly. Back at my computer, I imported the dozen or so snapshots into Photoshop and saved them all with meaningful names so I could easily find them.

To begin assembling your snapshots, chose one of the images as your starting point and open it in Photoshop. Choose Edit> Select All and then

Copy to place this image on your clipboard. Next, use the Eyedropper tool while holding down the Option key (Alt for Windows) to choose a color from your start image to be a neutral background color. Looking at your image, decide on how much bigger the canvas would have to be to assemble your basic elements together, and don't worry yet about what dimensions you want the final image to be. Choose File> New. With the dimensions of your start image loaded into the new file size, enlarge the dimensions of this document sufficiently to assemble your elements, select the Background Color option for Contents, and click OK. With your image still on the clipboard, select Paste to place your start image into its own layer and use the Move tool to relocate the position of your start image. Then, one at a time, open the other images that you want to include and use the Move tool to drag and drop them into the larger document (see Figure 6.12). Make sure to save your large file in Photoshop format as you go to preserve the layers.

To form transitions from one image to another, you'll need to create Layer Masks for each of your layers. With a layer selected in the Layers palette, click the Layer Mask icon. White will reveal a layer, black will mask it, and grays will blend your layer with the layers below. You can use the Gradient tool to create smooth transitions, make selections, and Delete to

**6.12** Choosing a starting image and a neutral background color, I created a new document large enough for assembling the snapshots and used the Move tool to bring them each into the large file and position them.

fill with the background color (Option[Alt]+Delete fills with the fore-ground color) or use any of your painting tools. You can review Chapter 1, "Compositing and the Creative Process," for help with masks, but remember that you can be loose and rough throughout most of this process (see Figure 6.13).

After your first version is flushed out, you'll probably want to make some substitutions from your collection of snapshots. At this stage I swapped in a different picture of my mom and used a Layer Mask to integrate it into the composition (see Figure 6.14).

Depending on how you'll be using the final image, at some point you might need to consolidate your composition. Make certain that your image is saved before you try to radically modify it. Use the Layers palette to hide and show various layers, and if you want to move multiple layers simultaneously, click in the Links column to link layers that you want to move together.

**6.13** Layer Masks smooth the transitions from one snapshot to the next.

**6.14** Along the way you can replace any elements with alternate snapshots.

I needed to make the image narrower to fit the proportions of the folding screen. Working first just by eye, I moved the layers around, hid some layers, and adjusted the masks until the composition was closer to the correct size (see Figure 6.15).

Then I checked the actual proportion that I needed for the screen and decided the best way to make the adjustments at this point was to increase the vertical canvas size. Choosing Image> Canvas Size, I chose the thumbnail representation that located the image in the center top and added the correct amount of space below the image (see Figure 6.16). With the canvas sized to the correct proportion, I moved things around a bit more to better fill the space.

To change the color cast or value of your image, choose an Adjustment Layer from the Layers palette and make any changes you want. I chose a Levels Adjustment layer to make the colors warmer and a bit lighter. If you want to include something in your image that you don't have in your collection of snapshots, try to fake it first to see if you really need it. To simplify my image, I wanted to eliminate some of furniture and try a rug in the foreground instead. Because I didn't have a snapshot of a rug handy, I just used patching techniques covered in Chapter 2, "Creative Problem Solving Using Layers," to assemble a fake rug out of different elements (see Figure 6.17).

**6.15** Moving layers and elements around so that the composition was closer to the right size.

**6.16** Using Canvas Size to set the actual proportions for the image and making more adjustments to the composition.

If you decide you like the composition as a stand-alone piece of art, you can experiment with ways to transform your collection of snapshots into something more cohesive. Using techniques similar to those in Chapter 5, I used Save As to save a flat copy of the image in TIFF format and then applied various filters and Blending modes to the flat version to make the image appear painterly (see Figure 6.18).

You might find that your composition moves in directions that necessitate your taking more photos. If you do need to keep working and have to incorporate new elements, make sure you return to the multi-layered file (without the effect applied). At this point in my process, the client had chosen a different direction for her screen, but I liked the composition myself and decided to show my mom. She really loved it but had some requests. The main change she wanted was (if we were to create a composition that she would actually hang in her home) to dress her up a bit. In addition she wanted me to substitute one of her own rugs for the fake one, and she even had some specific flower arrangements she wanted me to use. Because I had to photograph her rug and flowers anyway, I asked her to dress up in her outfit of choice. The flower arrangement wasn't on the table she liked, so back in the multi-layered file, I composited the new elements together using Layer Masks (see Figure 6.19).

**6.17** After applying a Levels Adjustment layer to change the color cast of the image and patching together a fake rug.

**6.18** Transforming snapshots into a more painterly look using techniques described in Chapter 5.

**6.19** Incorporating new photographs into the image.

If you have a number of elements that you always move together, you should probably create a Layer Set for them. I created a Layer Set for the table and vase with flowers so I could easily move them around as a unit. With the layers linked, choose New Set From Linked from the Layers palette pop-up menu. You can then attach a Layer Mask to the Layer Set so that the grouping can be integrated as a unit to the image below. If you need to apply a color correction to the images within a Layer Set, make sure to change the Blending mode for the Layer Set to Normal (from Pass Through). To work on some of the layers within a set, expand the Layer Set and unlink elements that you want to exclude, but remember to link them later if you need them to be a unit again (see Figure 6.20). I needed to scale the table but didn't want to stretch the vase, so I unlinked the vase while I used the Edit> Free Transform command. Then after I applied the transformation, I relinked the vase and collapsed the view of the Layer Set. My mom wasn't happy with the pose that I'd chosen, so I went back to my collection of shots and found one similar to the original pose. I then had to go back and photograph one last time to capture details such as her floorboards, how the wall met the floor, and the side of the desk.

If at any point you want to again transform the look of your image, save a flat copy of your image and apply the filters and such to the flat copy. I used Save As to save a flat copy as a TIFF image and then experimented with new ways to transform this image. Chapter 5 covers the details of how I transformed the composition at this stage into a painterly image. Also covered in Chapter 5 is how, after reworking the layered file yet again, I could apply the same effects to the final, flattened file (see Figure 6.21).

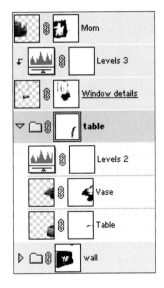

**6.20** Using Layer Sets to move related layers as a unit, and a section of the Layers palette at this stage.

**6.21** Chapter 5 covers how to create the final painterly effect, as well as how to apply the same effects to another updated file.

## Inserting Content into a Composition

By now you probably know that in Photoshop you can insert elements into a composition using Layers. You can control how each of the elements weaves into the composition by working into Layer Masks attached to each of the layers. You can organize multi-layered files using Layer Sets and attaching Layer Masks to those sets. The premise of this way of working is that you'll start by duplicating your original image. You'll then create a Layer Mask for the top version of your original image so that you can mask out the background elements and see through your foreground elements to the layers below. You can then insert new elements into the composition by working into layers you create between the versions of your image.

Sometimes you can simply begin to integrate new elements into a composition. With some compositions you might need to first make adjustments to integrate the new elements. Chapter 5 shows how I created a series of Etruscan figure images. The week after the September 11, 2001 disaster, while looking through this series, my heart stopped. To me, this version felt like the aftermath of a tragedy. Over the next few days I decided to rework it by incorporating the strange, cathedral-like lattice structure—all that was left of the World Trade Center. The image needed to be taller to accommodate the tower ruin, but I wanted to keep the figures the same size. After duplicating the layer with the original image, I added more space to the canvas size above the image (Image> Canvas Size). Using the Layers palette I hid the top duplicate, then selected the image of the figures on the Background layer using the Marquee tool. I chose Edit> Transform, and stretched the background image to be taller (see Figure 6.22).

Showing the top image duplicate again, I clicked the layer name to activate it then attached a Layer Mask by clicking the Layer Mask icon. To blend the original figures in the foreground with the stretched background, I painted into this Layer Mask with black, white, and grays (see Figure 6.23).

After your basic composition is in place, you might need to clean up some of the areas where something shows through that shouldn't. In my image, the stretched figures in the Background layer were showing through. To

**6.22** The original image, then enlarging the canvas. I hid the top layer (a duplicate of the Background image) and stretched the orginal Background image.

**6.23** Showing again the top duplicate of the original, I created a Layer Mask to blend it with the stretched image below.

clean up areas, you can use a variety of patching techniques (see Chapter 2). I created a new layer above the others and used the Clone Stamp to patch the areas where the stretched figures still showed through.

When I first began to work on this image, I thought that I'd just create the tower on top, so I created a new layer on top and drew some dark shadows for the tower structure. You can continue to create new layers on top or underneath others so that the weaving in and out occurs throughout the construction of your composition. I decided to create separate layers for the lights of the tower, above the Darks layer (see Figure 6.24).

To work on layers together as a unit, you can link them by activating one of them and then showing the Links icon for the other layers in the Layers palette. If you want to continually work on them together, you can then put them into a Layer Set. To do this, choose New Set From Linked from the Layers palette pop-up menu. You can continue to add layers within a Layer Set by opening up the Layer Set (click the arrow to the left of the Layer Set) and then clicking the New Layer icon. I linked the tower layers together, using Free Transform to stretch them. I then placed them in a Layer Set. When I wanted to add more detail to the tower, I opened up the Layer Set, added a new layer, and then painted into it (see Figure 6.25).

**6.24** Creating the tower by painting into separate layers for the darks below the layers for the lights.

**6.25** The Layers palette and image shown after I created the first five layers, linked the tower layers and stretched the tower. The last image is shown after I placed the tower layers into a Layer Set and continued to work.

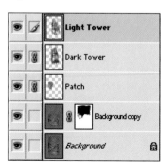

To control how sets of elements interact with layers below, add Layer Masks. To control how all the tower layers interacted with the background, I created a Layer Mask for the Layer Set by highlighting the Layer Set and clicking the Layer Mask icon. Then painting into the Layer Mask with black, white, and grays, I selectively painted where I wanted the tower to be visible (see Figure 6.26).

I wanted to make the tower more solid (in contrast to the ethereal figures) by applying a filter effect to just the tower. To do this I hid all the layers except the tower layers and then chose Edit> Copy Merged. I then pasted the copy on top, which created a new layer, Layer 6. To this merged (flat) copy I experimented with different effects and ended up with Filter> Emboss, using exaggerated settings of –120, 23, 304 (see Figure 6.27).

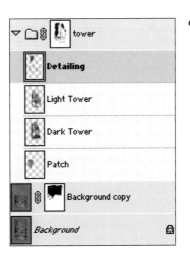

**6.26** After making a Layers Set from the linked layers (and creating a new layer within the set for detailing), I added a Layer Mask to the Layer Set to affect how the Layer Set would interact with the layers below.

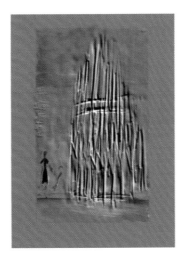

**6.27** After hiding all the layers except the tower layers, I made a merged copy, pasted the copy into its own layer, and then applied an Emboss filter to the merged copy.

I duplicated this Embossed Layer 6 a number of times, trying various Blending modes and Opacities and then reordering the layers. Linking all the embossed layers, I then created a Layer Set for them. Within the Layer Set I continued to experiment with duplicating the layers, reordering them, and adjusting the Blending modes and Opacities. The final Layer Set for the tower effect contained many sublayers set to different Blending modes, with all set to 100% Opacity. (For more about improvisational ways of working with Blending modes and Opacity, see Chapters 3 and 5.) I attached a Layer Mask to the Layer Set and painted into the mask to better blend the overall combined set into the layers below (see Figure 6.28).

To weave the figures in and out of the composition, I created a Layer Set for the background images (called "Fore" for foreground figures). After duplicating the Fore Layer Set, I placed one above and one below the tower layers. I then created Layer Masks for each of the Layer Sets and painted into them to control which layer was visible in each area. To finish the image I created a new layer and painted in my signature, and then used Layer Effects (from the Layers palette) to apply a Drop Shadow and Color Overlay. I also applied a few separate color corrections by choosing from

**6.28** Using nonlinear ways of working to create the final embossed effect, then creating a Layer Set for the embossed layers where I added more layers and attached a Layer Mask to better blend the embossed tower with layers below.

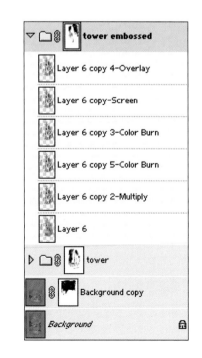

the Adjustment Layers pop-up in the Layers palette and then making the color corrections (one Adjustment applied only to just the signature layer). Lastly, I created a more neutral gray frame around the image and cropped the entire image using the Crop tool (see Figure 6.29).

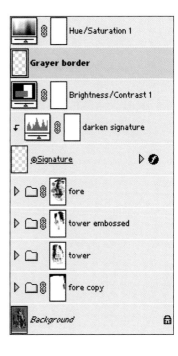

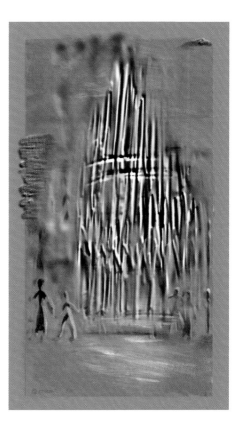

**6.29** The final image and the layers of "From the Ashes."

## More Exploration Suggestions

Use Lighting Effects and/or Adjustment Layers to explore possible changes in color direction for your composition.

Digitize a work from any other medium and try to figure out how you want to change it using Photoshop Painting and/or Compositing tools.

Use layers and Layer Masks to insert elements into an existing composition.

Create an imaginary space by assembling a series of digitized photographs. Try doing this with both photos that you shoot expressly for this purpose and with images you already have hanging around.

CHAPTER 7

# Creating Monotypes from Digital Images

There are numerous ways to create archival prints from your digital images. I create limited edition prints of my digital art and even use digital technology to reproduce my oil paintings in limited edition prints.

Limiting an edition won't transform digital prints into unique works of art; however, you can reinterpret digital images as unique works of art using a simple printmaking technique called *monotypes*.

If you're willing to experiment a bit with paints or inks, using prints of digital images as templates, you can create unique hand-printed mono-types. You can use any digital image as a template, including photo-graphs, collages, paintings or drawings. You can even make templates from digitized snapshots or scanned objects such as leaves or lace (to scan three-dimensional objects, drape a cloth over the objects on the scanner).

Four of the monotypes I made from
a digital snapshot.

Creating monotypes is not too complicated. Apply paints or inks to a surface of a piece of metal, glass, or plastic called a *plate*. Then place the moistened paper on the plate and rub the backside of the paper with a hard roller or spoon (or with a printmaking press, such as an etching press, litho press, or book press) peel off the paper and hang the print to dry.

If you're new to painting or printmaking, this can serve as a good introduction to monotypes and traditional materials. If you're already familiar with monotypes, I hope you'll be inspired to find new ways of integrating digital images into your printmaking process.

## Creating Your Digital Templates

To translate works from the computer as monotypes, you'll print out digitized images to use as templates. You can use templates to start you off in a general creative direction, to provide you with an exacting guide for creating very specific details, or to help you maintain the placement or shape of key elements while you focus on expressively playing with paint.

The process of printing your monotype reverses the image that you created; therefore, for a monotype to appear in the same fashion as your initial sketch or template, you'll need to flip the template and create your monotype image in reverse. After you print your monotype, it will reverse again and be oriented correctly. If you are using a Photoshop image as a template, you'll often want to begin the preparation of your image by choosing Image> Rotate Canvas> Flip Horizontally. So that you can see your digitally printed template through your plate, try using a transparent plastic, such as Plexiglas, or a glass plate (Figure 7.1).

You can choose to output digital images in the appropriate scale to match the plate size, or choose to have a plate made to fit a particular image.

If you're just starting out, I recommend that you begin relatively small. Working small allows you to see faster results, requires less workspace, and saves you money on materials. I had a number of Plexiglas plates made ranging in size from a 6" square to 9" by 12" and used a 6" square plate for all images in this chapter. For monotypes using these small plates, I tend to choose more atmospheric subjects with less emphasis on detail.

**7.1** The template is printed from the computer and then placed beneath the transparent plate.

Most hardware stores and glass replacement shops will cut plastic or Plexiglas to whatever size you want. If the edges are at all sharp, use a wood file to round off the edges and corners so they don't cut you or cut through the paper when you print. If you decide to use glass, make sure that you choose a glass sufficiently thick so it doesn't break under the pressure when printing, and make sure that the glass shop smoothes all edges and rounds all corners so you won't cut yourself. Plexiglas is the best plate to use with a press to avoid the shattering of glass under heavy pressure. The paper will receive more ink when a press is used. The edges of the Plexiglas plate must be filed before using a printing press and to avoid cutting through the felt blankets used to cushion the plate as it passes through the press.

When using a spoon against the back of the paper, be sure to rub in a consistent fashion to achieve the best image. Soft papers with high absorbency, such as rice paper, are best to use without a press; when you use absorbent paper, your image will transfer more easily from plate to paper. This printing process is similar to printing a woodblock.

## Customizing Your Image

Before you embark on an ambitious work, you might want to make some tests to gauge the limits of the medium and to become comfortable with the pigments, papers, and the process itself. Pigments that are too thick will squish around when you print them or might create a tear as you lift the paper away from the plate. Pigments that are very thin won't be visible on some papers but might be fine on others. If you layer pigments, the last on the plate will be printed behind the previous marks. Experiments are essential also to discover how much detail you are able to convey (it might be less detail than you think) and whether you need to simplify your imagery (Figure 7.2).

**7.2** Experiments with different kinds of mark-making on the plate; the first was somewhat thin, wet pigment, and the second was thicker pigment and quite dry.

**NOTE**

If you do want to try some test monotypes before choosing an image, skip ahead to the "Preparing Your Work Area" section later in this chapter and then return here when you're ready to prepare an image to be used as a template.

After you've chosen both your image and a specific size plate, you might want to crop the image to match the plate's proportions. Use the Crop tool, set the Width and Height Options to match your plate, and keep the Resolution field blank. You'll then be able to adjust the crop area and location while maintaining the proportion. Press Return or Enter when you are pleased with the crop.

To help me get started in a creative direction, I'll often make adjustments to an image that I intend to use as a template. After I chose a 6" square Plexiglas plate for a monotype of a cluster of flowers, I imported a digital snapshot of flowers into Photoshop. I next used the Crop tool (holding down the Shift key to constrain the crop to square dimensions) to find a

composition I liked and applied the crop. I then resized the image to fit
the plate using Image> Image Size (with Resample Image disabled). I
entered 6 (inches) and clicked OK. To create a more graphic (and less
photographic) look for my flowers, I experimented a bit with layers and
Adjustment Layers. At the end, I had created two duplicates of the Background layer. To the middle duplicate I applied Filter> Gaussian Blur. On
the top layer, in the Layers palette, I set the Blending mode to Overlay.
To make the image a bit richer, I chose Levels from the New Adjustment
Layer pop-up and then clicked OK without making any adjustment. Still
in the Layers palette, I set that new Adjustment Layer to Multiply and reduced the Opacity until I liked the result, which was 34% (Figure 7.3).
(For more about improvising with layers, see Chapter 3, "Improvising
with Color Using Layers.")

**7.3** To inspire a direction for the monotypes, I experimented with layers to create a more graphic look for the flowers.

Sometimes when I'm preparing a template, I simplify it by covering areas
that I find distracting. I initially tried to create a template made from my
Angels painting by just resizing the height to fit within my plate. But after
making a few unsuccessful prints, I decided to alter the template by eliminating all but the foreground angel and centering the remaining angel
larger within the plate. In Photoshop, I cropped the angel's image to
match the square dimension of my plate using the Crop tool (holding
down the Shift key). To simplify the composition, I used a series of layers

**NOTE**

You can use the Clone Stamp tool in the layers above to retouch photos. To better blend the retouched layer to the layers below, attach a Layer Mask so you can selectively airbrush where the retouching should appear.

above the image to patch over what I didn't want. In some layers I painted using the Airbrush or Paintbrush. Other layers were created when I copied and pasted areas from other parts of the image. I moved around the copied patches so they covered areas and used Layer Masks to determine which portions were visible. With other pasted patches I used the Edit> Transform command to enlarge, stretch, rotate, or flip it (Figure 7.4). (For more about patching techniques, see Chapter 2, "Creative Problem Solving Using Layers.") Considering I was only using this patched version as template, I wasn't terribly concerned about making it look perfect and instead created the simplified version quite quickly.

If you make no other changes, in most cases you'll probably need to resize the image to fit the plate you've chosen. To resize the image without changing the quality of the image, choose Image> Image Size and make sure that the Resample Image option is disabled. Depending on the size of your plate, you can now enter a new height or width. The corresponding dimension will automatically adjust, keeping the correct proportion of your image.

In the process of printing the image from plate to paper, the image reverses (Figure 7.5).

**7.4** After scanning an oil painting into the computer, I resized it to fit within the 6" plate I'd chosen. I then simplified, cropped, and enlarged the image.

**7.5** A painting on a Plexiglas plate, and the resulting print with the image reversed.

If the orientation of the composition is critical, often printmakers reverse the initial development of the plate. By reversing the image in the initial creation, when it is printed, the process of transferring from plate to paper will reverse the reversed—yielding a correct orientation of the final print. Thankfully, reversing images is very simple on the computer. Before you print out your template, in Photoshop choose Image> Rotate Canvas> Flip Horizontal.

## Variations on the Theme

There is another way to reverse a template besides flipping it in the computer. Many printers come equipped with sample media for test prints, and one of the samples is often a clear or transparent film. Used primarily with overhead projectors, clear film also can be great for printing monotype templates. Film is more durable than paper, and the side without ink can even be lightly cleaned.

I began creating monotypes from digital images because of one particular project. I was commissioned to create a drawing of a home (called

"The Point"), but I ended up digitally compositing a number of drawings (see Chapter 1, "Compositing and the Creative Process," for details on this project). Instead of delivering a final drawing, I presented the client with a digital print. Though the client was pleased with the print, I wanted to provide her with an authentically original artwork as well. She was very particular about the placement of the house in relation to the rocks, the trees, and the water, so instead of starting again from scratch, I decided to use the drawing that she had already approved as a template. I resized the print to fit the plate using Image> Image Size, entered the plate size for Width, kept the Resample Image option disabled, and clicked OK (Figure 7.6).

NOTE
You can take a tip from the printmakers: Most printmaking studios have a mirror readily available for a quick reverse view of an image or printing plate.

Because it was a particular view of a landscape, it was essential that I not reverse the final composition. For the final to be correctly oriented when it was printed, I needed to create the monotype in reverse. To help me to work in reverse (something I find challenging), I made two prints: a transparent print to use as a template and a paper print to keep as a visual reference when the template became covered with paint.

For the version to use as a reference, I reversed the image using Image> Rotate Canvas> Flip Horizontal and printed it out on regular paper (Figure 7.7).

**7.6** The composited landscape, resized to fit the plate.

**7.7** Using Image> Rotate Canvas> Flip Horizontal to reverse the image printed on paper.

If you intend to print on film instead of paper, *don't* reverse the image, but instead print the image correctly and then physically flip over the transparency. Flipping over the transparency will reverse the image and place the ink side of the print down (away from your plate), which will protect the ink side from pigments and liquids. If the exposed side of your template gets wet or dirty, you'll be able dry it off or even lightly clean it. You can print directly on Mylar with some laser and inkjet printers. Check your printer specifications in terms of printer media before attempting this.

When you flip over the template, place it on top of a piece of clean, white paper so you can see the template clearly. Use inexpensive paper under your transparent template and change it if it gets dirty.

Because there was no visible edge to the image within the template, I used a permanent marker to make four registration dots, one marking each corner of the plate. I could consistently maintain the registration of the plate within the template by placing the plate within the registration dots (Figure 7.8). You also can print using crop marks to help you with positioning.

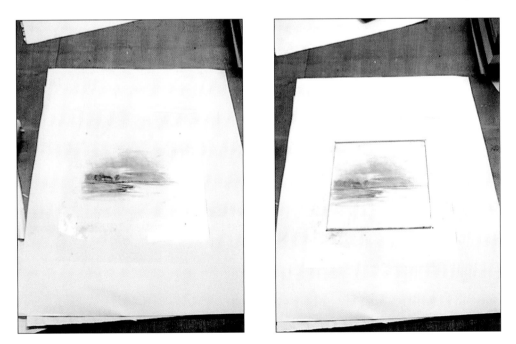

**7.8** After printing the digital landscape on transparent film, it's flipped over and placed on top of white paper with the transparent plate on top. Small black dots made with a marker create registration marks for the plate within the template.

## Preparing Your Work Area

If you don't have access to a printmaking studio, you'll need to prepare an area with a clear surface for printing monotypes.

You can be economical with space. When I'm working on small plates, my entire printing studio fits on a five-foot worktable with a sturdy clothesline behind my work area to dry the finished prints.

If you don't have an area large enough for everything together, you can set up separate small areas for painting (messy) and one for printing (clean). If you're working in oils or permanent inks, to prevent damage by stains or solvent, thoroughly protect the surfaces for your painting area with plastic and then put newspaper on top (so it's not too slippery).

See the section, "Some Final Notes on Materials," for detailed tips and suggestions on papers and pigments.

Within my little five-foot printmaking studio, I've delineated five different work areas (Figure 7.9). Here are my suggestions for your simple printing studio setup:

1. **An area for you to paint on your plate**. This area might get messy, and your paints or inks should be nearby. I wear rubber gloves when I paint then take them off when I handle clean paper and print. If you don't wear gloves, make sure your hands are clean whenever you handle the paper.

2. **A container that holds an inch or so of clean water, large enough to submerge your paper.** If you have a very clean sink with a stopper nearby, this can work just fine. I don't have running water or a sink in my studio, so I put some water in a large plastic tub that was supposed to organize junk in a closet. If you use a metal or plastic tub, you can easily place this on the floor or somewhere removed from the inking area.

3. **An area to blot the paper before you print**. If too much water is left on the surface of the paper, it will not absorb the oil-based inks in those areas, or it will bleed the watercolor inks. The paper should be

dampened and dried uniformly to a consistency that works best. For best results, use large blotter paper. I use dishtowels—they contain less lint than bath towels—and clean paper towels, which you can keep drying and reusing. The blotting area should be clean and near the water container; both should be set apart from the printing and inking area. I make two stacks of dishtowels, place a clean dry paper towel onto one stack, put down the print paper, and then cover it with another paper towel and the second stack of dishtowels. Pat the pile to blot the paper. When you remove the top pile of dishtowels, if necessary, blot with another dry paper towel. For smaller paper you can use one stack of towels folded in half to blot the paper.

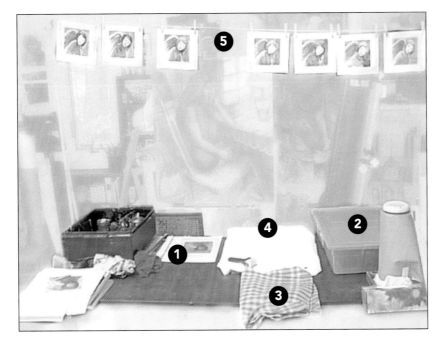

**7.9** The different areas of my printing studio.

4. **An area for you to print.** If you don't have a printmaking press, you'll need a clean, dry area. I put the printing material on a piece of stiff board so I can stack it over the tub of water if I need the workspace while I'm inking or storing my printmaking stuff. (See the next section, "Centering Your Print Within the Paper," for details on how to align the paper to your plate.)

5. **A line and clips for hanging your prints to dry.** I used to tack up prints on a board, but they tended to buckle when drying. I now prefer a clothesline and clothespins. Make sure the line is sturdy— damp paper weighs more than you think! If possible, give yourself enough room to hang a batch of prints at once. To prevent wrinkling, hang the pins so that they can slide along the line and so as the print dries, the pins can move.

## Centering Your Print Within the Paper

This is a quick trick, and you should prepare an underlay or registration paper before you begin to ink or paint your plate.

Whether you are using a press or printing by hand, this method will help you align your paper with your plate. Take a clean piece of cheap newsprint or drawing paper (acid-free is great) larger than the paper that you'll be using for printing. Place a piece of your printmaking paper squarely within the larger drawing paper, and with a pencil lightly mark off each corner of the paper. Then take your clean plate and center it within the pencil marks that you've just made. Now, mark each corner of the plate (Figure 7.10). These setup marks will create a better print if you take the time at this point to measure the margins between the paper size and the plate.

**7.10** So that you'll be able to align the paper to the plate when printing, you should mark where the paper will go and where the print should align within the paper.

When it's time to print, you'll align the plate within the inner four corner marks. Then place the paper on top, aligning it carefully with the outer corner marks. (Hint: I find it easiest to line up the paper with the top two marks and slowly lower the paper down over the plate to align with the lower marks.)

## Painting and Printing the Plate

When your studio is ready, take your template, place it in your painting area, and then place your transparent plate over the template. With your template as a guide, paint or apply ink to the plate. You can use brushes, cloths, paper towels, or sponges to apply ink or paint. You can use rollers to coat the plate, though as you cover the plate, you won't be able to see your template. Use brushes, cloths, or paper towels to wipe off the ink selectively or to wipe the plate clean and start over again. It's important to remember that anywhere on your plate without pigment will remain the color of the paper. You also can selectively wipe out areas to produce highlights or to ensure white areas. Cotton swabs are good for cleaning small spots, as well as adding dabs of ink to repair the image in process on the plate.

To create a color monotype of "The Point" landscape image, in addition to the template and a duplicate of the template (so I could refer to it as the template became obscured with pigment), I also keep a couple of color reference photos of the image nearby. These color photos were shot and chosen by my client because they represented a color, cast, and mood that she particularly liked. By using a print of the composited drawing as a template under my plate and a print beside me (while having the photos for color inspiration), I was able to concentrate on the color and the gesture of the painting, while easily maintaining the placement of key elements (Figure 7.11).

When you're ready to print, if necessary carefully clean the edges of the plate with a cloth or paper towel. Then place the plate onto a clean piece of registration paper within the marks that you've made for the plate (see the previous section if you need help).

**7.11** The inked plate (still on top of the transparent template) shown with one of the color reference photos.

Using clean hands, make sure that your paper is soaked (it should have been soaking in clean water for at least a few minutes and up to an hour or so). Blot the paper dry until you don't see any visible water.

Then align the paper to the outer four corner marks of the registration paper, carefully placing the printmaking paper on top of the plate.

If you have access to a printmaking press, follow the protocol for using the press. Because I didn't have a printmaking press in my studio, I used a hard roller (purchased in an art supply store) to transfer the painting to the paper (Figure 7.12). To print by hand, hold the paper in place with one hand and roll hard with a roller or rub with the back of a metal spoon from one side to the other, methodically covering the entire plate.

With some papers you'll be able to see the image through the back of the paper as you print. You can carefully lift a corner of the paper to make sure that you've pressed hard enough. (It's always better to press too hard than not hard enough.) When you're ready, slowly lift off the paper from the plate and hang it with clothespins to dry. The printmaking term is called *pulling a print*.

**7.12** The resulting printed monotype.

Often a small amount of ink is left on the plate after printing. This remaining ink is called a *ghost*. If you have enough of a ghost on a plate, you can print the plate again, or you can use the ghost as a guide for your next inking—some printmakers prefer the second or third monotype print from a plate. Of course you can always wipe off the ghost to start again with a clean plate.

I emailed snapshots of the first round of monotypes to the client who requested a more serene interpretation. After about 20 monotype prints using the landscape template, I finally printed one that we both liked (Figure 7.13).

**7.13** The final monotype presented to the client.

## Searching for Unlikely Subjects

Chances are you probably have an image hanging around just waiting to be interpreted as a monotype. Maybe it's something out of focus, cropped strangely, or is a salvaged fragment from something long discarded. Sometimes the best subjects for monotypes are images that you've put aside.

A number of years ago, I took a couple of pictures in the Etruscan Museum in Rome. In one of the glass cases there were marvelous groupings of iron figures that reminded me of sculptures by the artist Giacometti. I didn't know the proper way to photograph through a glass case with my point-and-shoot 35mm Olympus camera, so I took three shots: one with a flash and two without. Although the flash gave me a better representation of the figures, something magical happened to the other two shots (Figure 7.14).

For years these snapshots just floated around my studio. Then recently while I was making some monotype prints, I suddenly remembered these snapshots. I decided to make a series of gestural monotypes from the final photographic image. After resizing a scan of the photo in Photoshop so it fit horizontally within my Plexiglas plate (using Image> Image Size), I printed it on transparent film. Flipping over the transparent template, I placed the Plexiglas plate on top and completed a number of monotypes of the Etruscans (Figure 7.15).

**7.14** Three snapshots of Etruscan figures in glass cases—the first with the flash and second two without. The last image (bottom-right) is the one I ended up working with.

**7.15** After resizing a scan of the photo in Photoshop to fit horizontally within my Plexiglas plate, I completed a number of monotypes of the Etruscans.

After printing a number of versions of the figures, I decided to try printing on different colored papers. Remember that areas left without pigment on the plate remain the color of the paper. The ochre paper with visible fibers was interesting, but printing on black paper presented a wonderful opportunity. Because the original figures were dark, I used the template to paint around the figures, leaving the figures entirely unpainted. When I printed the plate, the unpainted figures became the color of the paper—in this case black (Figure 7.16).

**7.16** Two prints emphasizing the areas of the plate without pigment, which remain the color of the paper.

## Some Final Notes on Materials

There are an infinite variety of materials you can use. For the pigments you can use water-based inks or paints, oil-based paints, printmaking inks, as well as offset inks; for paper you can experiment with a wide range of printmaking papers.

In terms of permanence, I recommend using 100 percent rag (cotton), acid-free printmaking paper. If you are going to be hand-printing (versus using a printing press), it's generally easier to use thin to medium weight papers. You'll want your paper to be two to four inches (at least) larger than your plate in all dimensions—so you'll end up with a two to four inch margin of clean paper around your plate. I tend to use a straightedge or ruler and tear the paper, which gives the paper softer edges. You can experiment with colored paper, textured paper, and paper with more or less absorbency as well.

For pigments, a greater viscosity of oil in the inks, or moisture in the water-color paints, will ensure an easier transfer from plate to paper. Water-based paints dry quickly, so they are a bit trickier to use for monotypes. If you want to use water-based paints, be prepared to experiment with adding moisture to the plate as you work (some use a fine mist of water) or look for a book or a workshop on creating water-based monotypes. There are some ink extenders or mediums that help keep water-based inks from drying quickly. Water-soluble oil paints work just fine for monotypes, as do printmaking inks. Because my medium of choice is oil paints, I simply use my oil paints for monotypes as well. To minimize staining of paper by the oil medium in the paints (imagine dropping some cooking oil on a piece of paper), I thin my paint with turpentine-like substances and avoid linseed and other oil additives. Be aware, any oil-based pigments might actually yellow unprimed paper.

## More Exploration Suggestions

Alter an image or photograph to inspire a specific direction for a monotype and then print out the alteration as a template.

Experiment with different monotype techniques on your plate. Try testing different strokes that are wet, dry, small, large, stippled, and fluid.

Try printing monotypes on different colored paper and experiment with leaving areas of the plate without pigment.

Print a second ghost image remaining on a plate after printing the first, then work over the print with pastels, paints, inks or pencils. If your pigments are oil-based, use oil-based inks or paints or pastels over the ghost.

See if you can double-print one monotype over another print (be mindful about the alignment and what you are hoping to achieve!).

Experiment with other ways of making unique prints from a digital image: Print your digital image on paper or canvas and try to work over it with pencils, paint, or pastels when the image is wet or after drying the print.

Use the monotype process to enhance any image created on the computer. If you are successful, you will eventually discover a way to turn computer images into another dimension or edition of prints.*

*This exploration suggestion from printmaking technical editor Sandra Olenik.

CHAPTER 8

# Collaborating with Other Artists
## or Photographers

Unlike the performing arts, creating visual art is often a lonely profession. If you're weary of working alone or are simply intrigued by the prospect of collaborating with others, the computer can provide you with a creative medium in which collaborations of all sorts are possible. By creating our work using the computer, we as artists and photographers can experiment with each other's art without risk of damaging the originals. We can combine imagery without regard to the normal technical limitations of combining certain media. With Photoshop, painters can now integrate photographs into their work, and photographers can combine their images with work from other artists and photographers.

Because most of my creative life is spent alone, I welcome opportunities to collaborate with others. Through collaborations I am able to do much more than just incorporate photographs or works by others into my work; I can explore creative directions that I would never arrive at on my own.

Using Norma Holt's photographs and my hands operating the computer, our collaborative working process stretches us both creatively.

Though I normally collaborate with close friends and family, you can set up working relationships with anyone as long as all participants agree to establish common goals. This chapter includes examples of work that photographer Norma Holt and I have created together over the years. Although our collaborations have been very successful, Norma told me about a collaboration with another artist that was quite a disaster. Her problems could have been avoided or rectified if, in advance of their working together, they had had a written agreement outlining the parameters of their collaboration. To avoid such pitfalls yourself, it's a good idea to draft an agreement that addresses the goals that each person has for the collaboration. In this agreement, make sure you consider the attribution of credit for each of the participants, how you'll determine which pieces are successful, what will happen to the pieces that you don't unanimously approve of, and how the successful work will be used, shown, and sold.

One of the reasons I believe so deeply in collaboration is that I respect the dedication that each professional brings to his field. I consider myself a good amateur photographer, but the reality is that I spend much more time drawing and painting than I do taking pictures. Someone devoted to photography is likely to bring a depth to her work that I might never achieve. By all means, don't stop stretching to expand your skills and interests, but do look for opportunities when your project would benefit from a collaborative relationship with an expert who complements your skills and sensibilities. If you find yourself torn between settling for an unsatisfactory result or giving up on an idea altogether, consider inviting someone with the skills you're lacking to contribute his work or input. I truly believe that when people each contribute what they do best, there exists a potential for a much more powerful and successful final result than could have been achieved with one person alone.

## Establishing a Collaborative Relationship

You can establish collaborative relationships with anyone who is open to working with you. You might see an image that inspires you to approach the artist with the suggestion of collaborating, or your relationship with someone might precede the idea of collaboration. In the case of my work with photographer Norma Holt, our relationship preceded the idea of collaboration by more than 20 years.

We met when I was six. I lived downstairs from Norma, who was a portrait photographer. If I arrived home from school before my mother, I'd run up to visit with her—she worked out of her apartment. Norma became my "upstairs mother" Norma, and though we moved away a year later, I was one of Norma's frequent subjects; she photographed many of my passages of life (Figure 8.1).

By the mid-eighties, Norma had given up commissioned portrait photography and was instead traveling the world, photographing impoverished women and children. In 1990 while in town for an exhibit of her photographs, Norma visited my studio. She looked at my paintings and drawings but was particularly intrigued by what I was doing on the computer. In those days I was using a computer painting and photo-manipulation program called ColorStudio (created by the folks who also brought us the Painter program), and I'd just begun to experiment with incorporating stock photos into my computer painting. There was such a stark contrast between the content-rich work that Norma had been working on and the photo collages that I'd been creating in ColorStudio that we both began to brainstorm about collaborating (see Figure 8.2).

Norma and I set a date for her return, and soon we were at my computer with a handful of beautiful silver prints from her most recent show. We scanned them into the computer and began working. Norma had never touched a computer (and still hasn't). Starting with scans of her photographs, I was the designated driver with my hands on the computer, manipulating the images. Everything we did then can now be easily done in Photoshop.

**8.1** Photograph by Norma Holt of Sharon at age six.

**8.2** In 1990, the contrast in content between my early photo-collages and Norma's photographs is startling.

## Different Ways of Working Collaboratively

There were basically three different ways in which we have worked, and these parameters can apply to most collaborations that you're likely to encounter. The first is what I call "being the hands of another." There have been a few pieces for which Norma had very specific ideas about what she wanted. She would explain what she envisioned, and I'd try to figure out how to achieve it for her. This process is something that most of us are more familiar with. If you have ever worked to the specifications of an art director, then you're familiar with this process. Although inevitably your creative input will have an impact on the final piece, the direction of the image is coming from someone else. For this photograph of an "untouchable" mother and child in India, Norma had a newspaper clipping that she wanted superimposed. The sepia tone and exactly how the newspaper text was incorporated evolved organically as a collaboration as we worked (see Figure 8.3).

The second is what I call "true collaboration." For these images, we would both contribute to and direct the creative process. One of us would make a suggestion, respond to how those looked, and then continue to work from there. For me, this is the most exciting way of working, as the results often stretch my instinctive creative boundaries. This way of working is what we will explore further in this chapter. Sometimes we start with Norma explaining the situation to me, as in this photo that she took of a boy and his grandmother on the Mayan peninsula of Mexico. We talked about the contrast between the despair and poverty that Norma had photographed with the regal intricate carvings of the Mayan Empire. After coloring the image, I drew a Mayan figure and used a Relief filter to make it look more like a carving. Using semi-transparent masks I combined the two images as shown in Figure 8.4 (see Chapter 1, "Compositing and the Creative Process," and Chapter 3, "Improvising with Color Using Layers," for examples of how this can be done).

**8.3** The first image that we created together was under Norma's direction—with some collaborative decisions along the way.

**8.4** Norma's original photo, and our collaborative image, "Mayan."

Another example of this way of working was with a photo of West African market women from Burkina Faso. Norma wanted to create an image that contrasted the western way of life with the realities of hauling water and mere survival by these women. I was struck visually by how tall and elegant these women were. I wanted to exaggerate their stature, so I stretched the image. You can use Image> Image Size (disabling Constrain Proportions), or you can choose Image> Canvas Size, enlarge the canvas, and then use Edit> Transform to stretch the image visually. Norma then suggested that a movie poster with the theme of love might provide the needed irony. Using masking and coloring techniques, I drew in the poster (Figure 8.5).

The final way of working involves getting permission to work with someone else's images. Norma allows me to continue to play and explore with her images even when she's not here to give her input. These are still collaborations; the work has evolved from and uses her imagery. The

**8.5** Norma's original photo of Burkina Faso women, and our image, "Balancing Act."

elegance of the women in "Balancing Act" made me want to work with them some more. If removed completely from their lives, these elegantly tall women could even be runway models (Figure 8.6). The resulting image, called "Balancing Act II," was created with coloring techniques that still allowed the original image to exist behind the scenes (see Chapter 3).

Moving between these ways of collaborating is mostly a matter of where we are in physical proximity and what projects we're each working on. Sometimes Norma arrives with specific things that she'd like me to do for her, so we'll focus on my being her hands. If Norma is sitting beside me, I generally don't want to waste our precious working time together on projects that I could pursue on my own. In fact, I often won't take the time to actually finish the work while she's here. Instead, we'll get our collaborative work to a point where I am clear about what needs to be done to clean it up or finish it, and we then move onto another project to work on together.

**8.6** Continuing to work with the image on my own, "Balancing Act II" is really an extension of our work together.

## Collaborative Projects with Photoshop

In hopes of encouraging you to pursue collaborations of all sorts, this section will focus on a range of creative processes that Norma and I went through during our most recent collaborations and on how we arrived at our creative decisions.

Of course we worked in Photoshop this time around, but we also made some other adjustments to our working environment. For starters, instead of beginning with Norma's best work, as we did in 1990, this time Norma sifted through her flat files for prints that, for some reason or other, begged for something else to be done to them. Going through the stacks of prints that she had set aside, we chose a couple dozen images that we both responded to. We also upgraded our technical environment substantially. Instead of a scanner with a mere 16 levels of gray back in 1990, this time I sent the stack of Norma's prints that we chose to my service bureau for high-resolution grayscale and CMYK scanning.

### Enhancing What Is Already There

Not all images require complete transformation. Stay open to the concept of simply using Photoshop to enhance an image without necessarily radically changing it.

**NOTE**
To quickly fill your canvas or any selection with the Forground color, hold Option (Alt) and Delete. To fill the Background color hold Command(Ctrl) and Delete.

With her image of a Japanese monk, Norma wanted to enhance the sense of serenity. We started by increasing the size of the background behind the figure (Image> Canvas Size). After duplicating the Background layer containing the monk (dragging it over the New Layer icon), we filled the Background with black (with black as the Foreground color, hold Option[Alt] and Delete). Using the Move tool, we moved the photo around on the top layer until we were pleased with the placement of the monk in relation to the larger black canvas. Using the Lasso tool, I loosely selected the monk on his board and then clicked the Layer Mask icon to attach a Layer Mask. The Layer Mask preserved my selected area and masked the rest, allowing the black of the background to surround the monk. Then using painting tools, I worked black and white into the Layer Mask to refine what was visible in the original photo and what was masked. The final image eliminated many of the elements while surrounding the monk with a quite, serene, meditative black (See Figure 8.7).

**8.7** Slight, subtle changes to the image increase the serenity.

## Developing a Narrative

As you sort through possible images to work with, unrelated images might suggest fictional narratives. Whether the narrative is literal or conceptual, you can explore different ways to realize that narrative.

Both Norma and I loved a pair of images, taken years and countries apart, full of scratches and damage. We felt that both photographs spoke of loneliness and longing, so we decided to try and create a narrative of a mother and child. We explored many different ways of combining them using techniques discussed in the Chapter 1. Though there were a few that we liked, none were strong enough by themselves. By stacking three of them together, we felt that we had a composition that worked (Figure 8.8). We envision them printed large, perhaps taking up an entire wall in an installation.

## Struggling Through Different Ideas

The process of struggling through ideas that don't work is often an essential element of the collaborative process. Keep pushing, even when one of you are ready to give up—especially if one of you have a conceptual goal in mind.

**8.8** Norma's original photos, and the resulting collaborative image, "Motherless Child."

A colorful but somber photograph that Norma took never quite met her narrative expectations. It didn't seem to communicate the situation as fully as she wanted it to. These West African women were waiting for the food trucks to arrive, leaning tightly against a wall in the driving heat, hoping to find the shade thrown by the wall. Next to them stood the stick remains of what had once been a great shade tree. The photo still had Norma's black marker indications for where she wanted the lab to crop it, so in reworking the image we began by cropping it above the black mark (Figure 8.9).

Over the course of a couple of days, we tried many different, unsuccessful ideas in hopes of clarifying the narrative. I worked quickly and loosely, just trying to see if the concepts would work. We tried creating a luscious, painterly tree where the stick of a tree remained. We tried placing the tree outside of the wall. We tried raising the wall to dramatize the isolation using patching techniques discussed in Chapter 2, "Creative Problem Solving Using Layers" (Figure 8.10).

Norma was ready to give up, but I insisted on trying one more thing. I drew a tree on the wall. This got Norma interested again, and she asked if I could make the tree look as if it were once painted on the wall but had faded. In the Layers palette I set the tree layer to the Overlay Blending mode (Figure 8.11).

**8.9** Norma's original photograph.

**8.10** Two unsuccessful attempts to work on this image.

**8.11** A tree as if it were painted on the wall, then setting it to Overlay Blending mode.

Finally, I reduced the Opacity to 31%, created a Layer Mask for the painted tree layer (click the New Layer Mask icon), and painted into the Layer Mask with the painting tools (Figure 8.12). By painting into the Layer Mask, I allowed more of the wall from layers underneath to show through the tree painting and enhanced the effect that it had faded away (see Chapters 1, 2, and 3 for more about this way of working).

**8.12** For the final version called "African Memory," we reduced the Opacity of the painted tree to 31% and then attached a Layer Mask to further enhance the effect of fading the painted tree into the wall.

### Improvising and the Process of Discovery

Sometimes you'll find something to work with but don't know what you want to do or how to achieve it. Try everything. Use Save As frequently to save incrementally as you go and then experiment and make things up as you go along. If you need help structuring your improvisations, see Chapter 3, Chapter 4, "Radical Ways to Generate New Ideas from Older, or 'Finished' Work," and Chapter 5, "Nonlinear Creativity."

One of the photos that we both wanted to work with was of a woman in India going to the banks of the Ganges River to die (Figure 8.13). Flocks of people arrive daily as a religious pilgrimage to this river. We wanted to surround this skeletal woman by the spirits of this alley and bring the steps of the river to her feet.

The first thing I did was enlarge the canvas size so that black surrounded the photo where we wanted to expand the image. By choosing black as the Background color (press D to set the default Foreground to black and Background to white and then press X to reverse the Background and Foreground colors), the areas where the canvas was enlarged would be black. Choosing Image Size> Canvas Size, I used the thumbnail to place the image in the top center and added canvas to the sides and bottom (Figure 8.14).

**8.13** Norma's original photo.

**8.14** After enlarging the canvas with black as the Background color.

I created layers above and below the photo in which to work. Using techniques described in Chapter 2, I used the Clone Stamp tool to clone some areas of the image and then stretched and rotated copies of other areas to expand the image out into the black borders. Then attaching Layer Masks to each of the patching layers, I was able to paint into them with painting tools to control how the layers interacted with each other (Figure 8.15).

**8.15** Using patching techniques, I expanded the image into the borders and added Layer Masks, so that by painting into them I could control how the layers would interact.

After converting the image from Grayscale to CMYK (using Image> Mode), I created new layers. Into these new layers I painted the spirit figures and steps. Experimenting with different Blending modes, I set one of the steps layers to Hard Light, which created a glow (Figure 8.16).

To unify the image and increase the drama, I applied a sienna-hued Hue/Saturation Adjustment Layer (from the Layers palette) as shown in Figure 8.17.

Though I liked this image, Norma wasn't sure that it felt ghostly enough. I decided to keep pushing the image and try and realize what Norma had in her mind's eye. Removing the sienna hue, I created a new Hue/ Saturation, which darkened the image to a dark silvery hue. Attaching a Layer Mask to this Adjustment Layer, I used the painting tools to selectively remove the effect of the Adjustment Layer and bring back the light of the previous version of the image (Figure 8.18).

**8.16** Painting in the spirit figures and the steps, I then set the Steps layer to Hard Light Blending mode.

**8.17** Applying a Hue/Saturation Adjustment Layer.

**8.18** Applying a Hue/ Saturation Adjustment Layer and then using a Layer Mask for that adjustment to selectively remove its effect.

Finally, I decided to try combining multiple versions of the image together using Blending Mode changes. I made a merged copy of the layered file by choosing Edit> Copy Merged and then pasted it on top of all the layers. Experimenting with different Blending modes, I tried Hard Light. Before I did anything else, I used the Layers palette to hide and show various layers underneath this merged copy (Figure 8.19). Simply hiding the Hue/Saturation Adjustment Layer resulted in an effect that made Norma say "Stop! That's it!". Though the Hue/Saturation Layer had been essential in creating the merged copy, removing it after the copy was in place increased the contrast and enhanced the ghostly glow. Though I still like the sienna version, Norma feels that this second version is the definitive version of "The Steps of the Ganges." (For more about improvising with your work, see Chapters 3 and 5.)

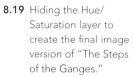

**8.19** Hiding the Hue/ Saturation layer to create the final image version of "The Steps of the Ganges."

## More Exploration Suggestions

Try and stretch your creative boundaries with your collaboration. If you are a photographer, collaborate with a painter. If you're a painter, collaborate with a photographer. If you're an expert in Photoshop, take on a partner who doesn't know anything about the computer. If you're new to Photoshop, you might want to find someone to work with who is more experienced than you, or you might want to find someone who can experiment along with you at the same level.

- Explore different ways of collaborating:

    1. Being the hands of another.

    2. Inviting true collaboration with full participation from each individual.

    3. Getting permission to explore work of another on your own.

- Use a variety of techniques to create your collaborative images, including something taken from techniques covered in each of the Chapters 1 through 7.

- Create collaborative works that involve very little change from the original as well as works that radically change the original images.

- Pursue a number of different directions from the same starting point. Experiment with combining the different results to see if they work together side by side or stacked on top of each other.

CHAPTER 9

# Simulating Installations of Your Work

There are many reasons to simulate installations of your work. You can see how a work would look installed in a specific place, in various locations, or how a number of different works would look in the same location. You can create presentations for clients or public works proposals. You can create simulations for purely self-promotional purposes. You can even use a simulation to help you make artistic decisions—seeing a sketch or digital work in the context of a space can help you decide at what scale the actual work should be produced.

Sometimes you'll want to create your simulation roughly and quickly. If you just need to run through a batch of possible images so your client can choose between installing an abstract mural or a miniature portrait in her hallway or if you can't decide which piece goes into which space, you'll want to work loosely and without much attention to detail. If instead you need to create a final image that will be included in a four-color corporate brochure, then you'll need to work in higher resolution and take the time to composite your images meticulously.

Simulated installations of paintings (top), a digital portrait as a mural (center), and the "virtual" relocation of a large stone and slate sculpture by Jill Sablosky placed into a landscape by the Glen Gate Company (bottom).

To create the simulations you'll generally need to composite digitized versions of your work and an image of a specific location. If you're new to compositing, please refer to Chapter 1, "Compositing and the Creative Process," for in-depth coverage on the technical details discussed in this chapter. Although the first projects will include a certain amount of technical detail, as this chapter progresses, projects will focus less on the technical aspects and more on the particular issues that illustrate the uniqueness of that project.

Simulating installations can become an integrated component of your creative process. If you get into the habit of viewing simulations of what you propose first, perhaps you'll be able to convince your clients to accept more challenging works. Being able to experiment with different ways of installing your work in Photoshop might even alter your ambitions for the scale of your final work. And ultimately, creating samples of your images as if they were installed can enhance your ability to promote your work and open up new marketing, granting, and exhibition opportunities.

## Overview of the Issues to Consider

After you've identified which works will be installed into which specific spaces, you'll need to determine the scale and resolution of your simulated installation. To create the simulation you'll then need to assemble and composite digitized versions of your images with your source locations.

Each project is likely to be unique, and therefore how you prepare the materials for each simulation will vary, but always use a high quality digitized version of your work to represent your work well. Next, ask yourself how will this simulation be used? Will it be used to create a 35mm slide, or will you just be emailing a low-res version to your client for approval? Is the space into which you'll be installing a critical factor in the simulation, or would you rather de-emphasize the space and focus the attention on the work itself? If you are going to be producing transparencies or high-resolution, four-color prints, then create your work at high resolution (300 pixels per inch or higher). If you are merely creating work to email for guidance on the direction of a project, then work more quickly in low resolution (72–150 pixels per inch).

## Two-Dimensional Images on a Flat Wall

Probably the least complicated installations to simulate are two-dimensional images, photographed straight on, and installed onto a wall photographed straight on.

For promotional purposes, I composited a number of photos of my painting studio to simulate a photo of my south studio wall (see Chapter 1 and Chapter 2, "Creative Problem Solving Using Layers," for details). After showing the printed version to a few people for feedback, I decided to replace a batch of the small paintings with some of my larger works. Instead of physically rearranging the paintings, reshooting, and recompositing those paintings, I decided to simulate the installation with digitized versions of the paintings. The scale of the studio composite was already determined and fairly high in resolution, so I would be scaling down the digitized paintings to fit within the space.

To place your work into a space, you might have to first prepare the space by moving or removing items. In my studio composite, I needed to relocate some of the original paintings and delete others.

I began by moving the entire right side of the studio to the right. Using the Rectangular Marquee tool, I selected chunks of the image (holding Shift to add more and Option[Alt] to delete), copied, and pasted. The pasted area was then in its own layer, which I then shifted over to the right using the Move tool while holding the Shift key. I wanted to remove some paintings entirely and replace those areas with a blank wall (Figure 9.1). I knew that I'd be placing new art in front, so to begin with I didn't work very carefully. In layers above the Background layer, I used techniques discussed in the studio project in Chapter 2 to patch the walls.

To relocate a painting, I selected it from the original Background layer using the Marquee tool and Edit> Copy. I clicked the topmost layer of patched wall and Pasted a copy of the painting, which would place it into its own layer, on top of all the others. With the painting in its own layer, I could easily relocate it using the Move tool. To blend the painting better with its new location, I added a Layer Mask and used the Airbrush tool to soften the transition from the old wall beneath the painting to the new wall below its new location.

**9.1** Selecting a section of the image, and then after moving it to the right, using patching techniques to remove some paintings and prepare a white wall.

I then used the Move tool to bring the new paintings into the studio image one at a time. After measuring the size of the new paintings in relation to the ones on the wall already, I used Edit> Free Transform (you can use Edit> Transform> Scale instead) to scale each of the paintings to the correct size within the space. Then using the Move tool again, I moved the new paintings in the locations where I wanted them to be.

After creating Layer Masks for the new paintings to isolate the paintings themselves, the edges of the new paintings were too crisp and harsh. So working into layers above the paintings, I alternated between the Painting, Clone Stamp, and Eraser tools to redraw and soften the edges. To create the edges I needed to draw in straight lines with the tools. To draw in straight lines with these tools, click where you want the line to begin, hold the Shift key down, and click on the other side of where you want the line to end. You can continue to Shift+click back and forth until you get the effect you like. For the shadows, I created layers between the painting and the wall (Figure 9.2). Sometimes I'd add a Layer Mask so I could more easily soften the transition from the shadow to the layer below. I'd use the Shift+click method in the Layer Mask as well.

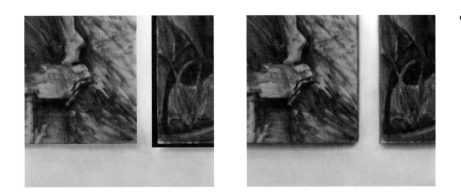

**9.2** Close-up of the edges and shadows of the new paintings before and after touch-ups, and the final simulated studio.

## Instant Framing

Photoshop's Layer Styles provide some great tools for simulating framing of your work. I discovered this when I was trying to show a client how one of my digital paintings would look in her hallway.

With a digital snapshot of the client's hallway and my art open and visible, I used the Move tool to drag my artwork into the hallway file. Using the Transform command (Edit> Free Transform or Command+T[Ctrl+T]), I sized the image and then adjusted the corners so the image appeared slightly in perspective. To distort your image to create a perspective look with Free Transform, hold the Command(Ctrl) key before grabbing a corner; you'll then be able to move that corner independently (Figure 9.3).

To frame the art I began by creating a gold border around it. To create a border around something, select it by Command+clicking for Mac or Ctrl+click for Windows on the layer containing the image. To round the corners of the frame, I created feathering for the selection. In the Options bar, for this low-resolution image I set the Feathering to 6 (feathering isn't applied until you act on the selection). To enlarge the selection to create the frame, I chose Select> Modify> Enlarge Selection and then entered 12 pixels. Now the selection was large enough to create the frame but included the artwork itself. To delete the artwork from the selection, I held Command+Option (Ctrl+Alt for Windows) when I clicked again on the layer containing the artwork. With the framed border alone selected, I created a New Layer and filled the selection with a gold color chosen from the image using the Eyedropper tool, as shown in Figure 9.4. (You can choose a color from the Colors palette.) A quick way to fill any selection with the Foreground color is Option+Delete for Mac, Alt+Delete for Windows.

**9.3** The original hall, and after bringing in the artwork, using the Transform tool to size and distort the art to simulate perspective.

**9.4** After filling the selected area with a gold color.

Choosing any Layer Style from the pop-up at the bottom of the Layers palette opens the Styles dialog box. From the dialog box I experimented with various styles and customized Bevel & Emboss, Drop Shadow, and Satin styles.

As this was too simple for the client's taste and the scale of the artwork, I used the same procedure and created a selection expanded to a total of 24 pixels. I created a new layer below the previous frame layer and filled the new selection with a lighter gold. I copied the effects from the first frame to the new one below using the Layers palette. Grab the Effects layer from any layer, hold Option for Mac (Alt for Windows), and drag the Effects layer to the new layer. To edit an Effects layer, double-click it. I made a number of adjustments to the Effects layer for the larger frame, including increasing the texture of the Bevel & Emboss effect. To better blend the two frames, in the Layers palette I hid the Drop Shadow effect for the inner frame (Figure 9.5).

**9.5** The initial frame, and then after increasing the texture of the Bevel & Emboss effect to create the final frame.

Then I decided that the entire art piece was too large for the space. To help me organize my file, in the Layers palette I linked the artwork and the frame layers and then chose New Layer Set From Linked from the Layers palette pop-up menu. I hid the background using the Layers palette and made a merged copy (Edit menu) of the artwork with frame. To create the smaller version, I clicked the New Layer Set icon to create a new set and then pasted the merged copy into its own layer within the new Layer Set. I then hid the Layer Set containing the original artwork and frame layers and showed the Background layer again. Activating the layer containing the merged copy, I used the Free Transform command to reduce the size of the framed artwork. Lastly, within the top Layer Set I then created an Adjustment Layer to warm up the colors overall, as shown in Figure 9.6 (choosing Levels from the Adjustment Layer pop-up in the Layers palette).

**9.6** The final layer structure, and the final framed installation.

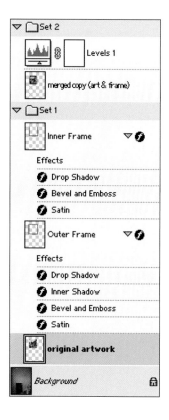

## Configuring Art to Fit a Space

Although you'll always want the highest quality reproduction to showcase your work itself, there are times when you might want to use lower resolution images for the backgrounds. If you're simulating an installation in which the emphasis is your work and not the specifics of the location into which you're installing, lower resolution backgrounds might be preferable. If you keep the background location in lower resolution and the artwork crisp and in higher resolution—although the viewer might not even be aware of this—images are emphasized and the background becomes less important.

For a series of state grant proposals, I needed to quickly create a number of examples of how I might install my work as mural projects. This particular series of grants was for public school buildings, so I concentrated on themes that I thought might be appropriate for schools. A colleague suggested that my small paintings of children's toys and dolls would be good subject matter for school projects if I could enlarge them to mural size. To apply for those projects I needed to produce samples of what such installations would look like.

I took a series of photos in a well-lit public building using my digital camera. I also scanned a sheet of 35mm slides of my doll and toy paintings using a transparency adapter for my scanner. To isolate the images within the slides from the black that surrounded them, I selected the images using the Marquee selection tool. As I worked, I used Shift to add to my previous selection, Option (Alt for Windows) to subtract from a selection, and Undo to return to my previous selection if I made a mistake. When all the images were selected, I pasted them into a new document. I chose Edit> Copy, made a new document (File> New), chose Transparent as the Contents option, and then Edit> Paste. To rearrange the images into a more orderly grouping, I'd marquee select an image and then use the Move tool to move that image to its new location (hold the Command key for Mac or the Ctrl key for Windows to turn the Marquee temporarily into the Move tool). I resized the canvas (Image> Canvas Size) and created guidelines to help me align the images (Figure 9.7). To make guidelines, show your rulers with View> Show Rulers and then click and hold within the ruler and drag down or in to create a guide.

The next step was to prepare the location images I had shot. I would eventually be creating 35mm slides of these simulations, so the first location shot needed to be cropped. The camera had been tilted, so I wanted to rotate it as well. I chose the Crop tool, and in the Options bar I entered 7 as the width and 10.5 as the height to match the proportions of a slide. I chose the area to crop by moving in the handles. To rotate the image, before applying the crop, I moved my cursor outside of the handles until it turned to a Rotate symbol and then grabbed the handle to rotate it so that the bounding box aligned with the floor tiles. To apply the crop and rotation, I pressed Return.

Because the art slides were scanned at a fairly high resolution, they would appear too large within the digital location shots. Instead of reducing the resolution of the art images, I would need to scale the location shots larger. Because scaling images larger in Photoshop can result in images appearing somewhat fuzzy, there are very few times when I recommend scaling images larger. However, when you want your artwork to be crisper and cleaner than the location image, it's fine to scale your location image larger.

**9.7** The original scanned slidesheet, the images after selecting, copying, and pasting them into a new document, enlarging the canvas, and lastly the arranged images shown with the guidelines.

To keep the file sizes down, I arranged the paintings in one file and would then bring the arranged paintings into the second file, which was the location shot. Before I began arranging paintings, I needed to figure out how much I needed to scale up the digital snapshot locations. With one of the painting files open I enlarged the Canvas Size to create more blank space around the painting (Image> Canvas Size). I used the Move tool to then bring the location image into this enlarged canvas. In the Layers palette I moved the Painting layer above the location shot (to move a Background layer above another layer, you can duplicate the Background layer by dragging it over the New Layer icon and moving the duplicate above the Location layer). I then clicked the Location layer and chose Edit> Transform. Using the Options bar, I kept entering percentages into W (Width) and H (Height), moving the cursor inside of the image to drag it around until the location seemed to fit the way I imagined in relation to the painting and wrote down the scaling information (Figure 9.8).

**9.8** The original snapshot, and a version enlarged using the Free Transform command in Photoshop, so that I could figure out how much I should be enlarging the actual one.

After canceling the transformation and deleting the Location layer, I was ready to resize the actual location file. Using the Image> Image Size command, make sure that the Resample option is enabled with Bicubic (the highest quality of the resampling options) and Constrain Proportions is selected from the pop-up. I chose 300-pixels per inch for the Resolution option, and in the Pixel Dimensions field I chose 500%. After saving this larger version of the location, I eliminated the backward word "Shalom" from the entryway by copying and pasting a blank part of the wall (Figure 9.9). For more about such patching techniques, see Chapter 2.

**9.9** The location shot after it was cropped, rotated, and resized to a higher resolution and retouched.

To arrange the paintings to fit within the location shot, I needed to see the exact shape and size of the space into which they'd be installed. In my newly resized location shot, I used the Pen tool to draw a path to define the area (holding the Shift key when I wanted to constrain lines to horizontals or verticals). To draw straight lines with the Path tool, click to place an anchor point that connects the previous anchor by a line and click the starting anchor point to close the path. If you're not familiar with the Pen tool, drawing curved paths can be tricky. The Photoshop User Guide offers some basic help with the Pen tool. If you need more help, I've developed a tutorial with QuickTime movies for the Pen tool in various programs; find the free demo as well as the full course at **www.zenofthepen.org**.

After you've created a path in Photoshop, you can save it by opening the Paths palette and double-clicking the working path. You can then rename it, and when you save the file, it will be saved with your image. (While earlier versions of Photoshop required you to save your working paths, recent versions of Photoshop will save your working paths for you.) After my path was saved, I'd use this path, and selections and masks made from this path, as a template for arranging my paintings, as well as to blend the paintings into the space at the end of this process (Figure 9.10).

**9.10** Using the Pen tool, I drew a path that defined the area into which I'd be placing my images. The Path palette with the saved path.

Paths can resize to fit the file you're pasting into; so to move the exact same-sized area defined by this path to my file containing the paintings, I first made a selection from the path. Hold Command for Mac or Ctrl for Windows and click a path in the Paths palette to turn it into a selection. You can drag and drop a selection marquee from one file to another, or you can save a selection as an Alpha Channel. Like paths, Alpha Channels can easily be turned back into selections. To save an active selection as an Alpha Channel, open the Channels palette and click the Save Selection As Channel icon. To turn an Alpha Channel back into a selection, hold Command for Mac or Ctrl for Windows and click the channel in the Channels palette.

For this simulation I dragged and dropped the selection from the location image to the file with the paintings, and then created an Alpha Channel in the painting file. To more easily view how the images in this file would look when cropped by the peak of the roofline, I used the Alpha Channel to create a triangle of white in the topmost layer (Figure 9.11). To use an Alpha Channel to make a masking shape, create a New Layer and then Command(Ctrl)+click your Alpha Channel to reload the selection. Next choose Select> Inverse to reverse the selection to all but your original selection. Press the D key to load your Default colors of black as Foreground and white as Background colors. To fill your current selection with your Foreground color, hold Option(Alt) while you Delete. To fill your selection with the Background color, hold Command(Ctrl) while you Delete. Deselect your selection with Command+D for Mac, Ctrl+D for Windows.

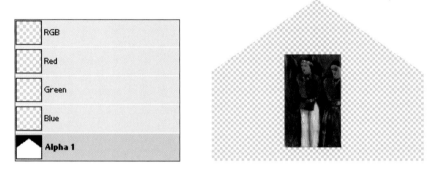

**9.11** Saving my selection as an Alpha Channel, and a masking shape shown with one of the images to determine scale.

Now that I could easily see the correct size of the space into which these paintings would be placed, I used the Move tool to bring the rest of the scanned paintings into this file one by one. I reordered layers (keeping them below the white masking object)—and by clicking on the appropriate layer—I could use the Move tool to move a particular painting to a new location. Alternatively, you also can try to enable Auto Select Layer in the Options bar, which will allow Photoshop to guess which layer you are trying to click (based on which image is below your cursor). After arranging the paintings, I again used techniques covered in Chapter 2 to patch areas that needed to be filled. And then creating Layer Masks, I masked some of the areas of paintings that were overlapping others. The final Layers palette shows a number of Layer Masks within this multi-layered file (Figure 9.12).

**9.12** The paintings in their final arrangement, after the patching and Layer Masks, and the final Layers palette.

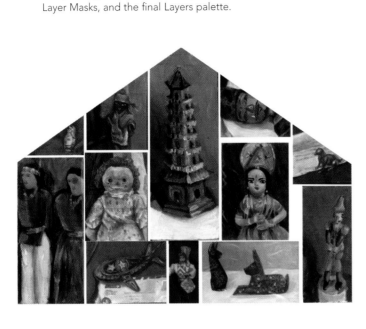

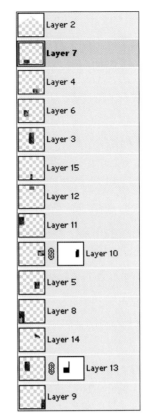

To copy a layered file as one flat image, hide and show any layers to create the version that you want to copy (for my version, I hid the white masking triangle layer). Next, make sure that your active layer is one of the visible ones, make a selection, and choose Edit> Copy Merged. I re-loaded the Alpha Channel as my selection (Command[Ctrl]+click the Alpha Channel) so I could make my merged copy of the images within the triangular shape. Now open your destination file. To make sure that the images that you'll be pasting align within this destination file correctly, first reload the selection you created in this file. If you've saved a path in this file, then reactivate your selection from the path; if you have an Alpha Channel, then use the Alpha Channel. In either case, Command+click for Mac or Ctrl+click for Windows on the path or channel to load it as an active selection. With this selection active, paste to create a new layer containing a flat copy of your layered file into the selected location (Figure 9.13). If you need to fine-tune the placement of the new layer a little, you can choose the Move tool and then use your arrow cursor keys to nudge the layer up, down, or side to side.

**9.13** The paintings pasted as one layer into the location image.

With the paintings in place, I needed to blend these images better into the background location. After adjusting the overall color and value of the background to better work with the paintings (choosing Levels from the Adjustment Layer icon in the Layers palette), I wanted to make the painting layer a bit richer. Using a way of working described in Chapter 3, "Improvising with Color Using Layers," I duplicated the Background layer and moved it above the other layers, experimented with different Blending modes, and chose Soft Light at 58% Opacity. To apply the adjustment just to the painting layer directly below it, I selected Option+clicked (Alt+click for Windows) the line between the Soft Light layer and the painting layer below to turn the layer above into a Clipping Layer for the layer below it (Figure 9.14). (Alternatively, you can create a Layer Mask for the Soft Light layer to isolate the application of the effect.)

To create shadows in the corners of the mural, I first activated the Alpha Channel by Command+clicking on it (Ctrl+click for Windows). To select only the outline itself, I created a border of the selection by choosing Select> Modify> Border and chose a pixel width. In a separate layer on top, I next filled the border with a dark color. So the shadow would blend with the image below, I set the Blending mode for that layer to Hard Light (Figure 9.15).

**9.14** After duplicating the layer with the paintings and changing the Blending mode and Opacity, I formed a Clipping Group with the Soft Light layer and the original version below.

**9.15** The active border selection, the darkened border shown alone, and the lightened border shown without the painting layers.

For final lights and darks, I used the original Alpha Channel to make a number of different layers. In one I used both the Edit> Stroke and Edit> Fill commands (which use your current tool and color settings). For other layers I used the Alpha Channel to create a Layer Mask. To make a mask from an active selection, click the Layer Mask icon. In one of the layers I used the Gradient tool to create a light to dark gradient, masking it with a shaped Layer Mask. In a couple of cases I did the reverse, created a shaped layer and made a gradient in the Layer Mask (Figure 9.16).

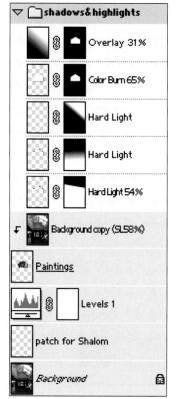

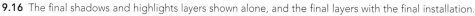

**9.16** The final shadows and highlights layers shown alone, and the final layers with the final installation.

Using similar techniques I installed a line of paintings into another snap-shot. I used the Free Transform command (Command+T for Mac, Ctrl+T for Windows) to distort the paintings into the space. Holding the Com-mand key (Ctrl for Windows), I was able to grab each of the corners individually and align the wall of paintings to the wall in perspective. I next rearranged the paintings a bit to better fit the space. Then I created a Layer Mask to mask out the paintings, so that they would be behind the banner (see Chapter 1 for more on Layer Masks).

To then put a painting on the banner, I used the Move tool to bring it into the composited file into its own layer. I then used the Free Transform command to distort the image to match the perspective of the banner (Figure 9.17). To patch the white background of the painting into the an-gled bottom of the banner, I again used techniques covered in Chapter 2.

**9.17** Putting a line of scanned paintings onto the angled wall using the Free Transform command, and a Layer Mask, and beginning to place another painting into the banner.

Attaching a Layer Mask to the layer containing the banner painting, I blended the painting to the banner using the painting tools in the Layer Mask. To make the painting part of the banner instead of floating on top, I experimented with various Blending modes for the Painting layer and chose Screen.

To finish this image I wanted to make the banner a bit brighter, so I duplicated the Screen layer and settled on Soft Light (Figure 9.18).

**9.18** The final Layers palette and the final image.

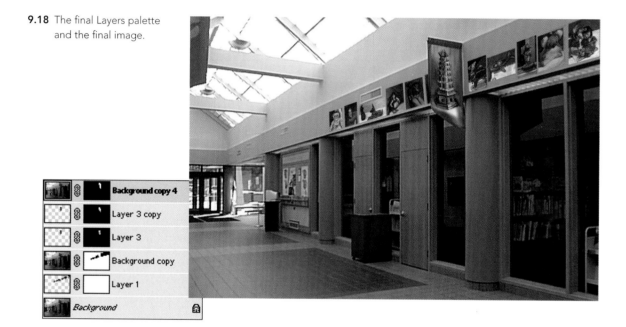

I also used very similar techniques for installing a group of paintings onto a gymnasium wall—with a few twists. As before I configured the artwork in a separate file, brought the artwork into the new space, and distorted it to fit. In this image though, the banister needed to be in front of the murals. To do this I used a technique covered in Chapter 6, "Compositional Brainstorming." Duplicating the Background image of the gym stairs, I moved the duplicate above the painting layer. I then attached a Layer Mask to the duplicate (click the Layer Mask icon), and carefully created a mask that would reveal the paintings below but would protect the banister. In addition to using painting tools, because the banister was made from exacting shapes, I used the Pen tool to outline some areas. After I had defined the area with the Pen tool, I activated the paths as a selection, and in the Layer Mask I filled the selection with white to mask.

To toggle the view of a Layer Mask between being invisible and a transparent overlay (so that you can see both the mask and the image), press the \ key.

To get the texture of the cinderblocks into the mural, I needed to overlay the original background on top of the image. Duplicating the Background Copy layer, I began by inverting the mask so that the blending effects would affect *only* the paintings and not the rest of the image. The easiest way to invert a mask (or any image) is to click it in the Layers palette, make sure that you don't have anything selected (Command+D or Ctrl+D), and then press Command+I for Mac or Ctrl+I for Windows. With the mask inverted, I experimented with the Blending modes for the layer. Duplicating that layer a number of times, I played with the effects of various Blending modes and Opacities on each of the layers. When I was done, I had three layers creating the overlay texture (Figure 9.19). For more about this way of working, see Chapter 3.

**9.19** The photo of the gym shown with the paintings in place with the mask seen as an overlay, and then the final layers and image.

## Improvising an Effect with Your Image

There were a few times when I knew that I wanted to alter an image but didn't know what I wanted to do. Using techniques described in Chapter 3, I improvised with Adjustment Layers and Blending modes to create variations that worked with the space.

To install my digital portrait of Louis Armstrong in a piano room, I ended up creating a sepia-toned effect (Figure 9.20).

**9.20** The original piano room, and the digital portrait of Louis, and then the sepia-toned portrait installed into a more richly colored space using Layer Masks and Adjustment Layers.

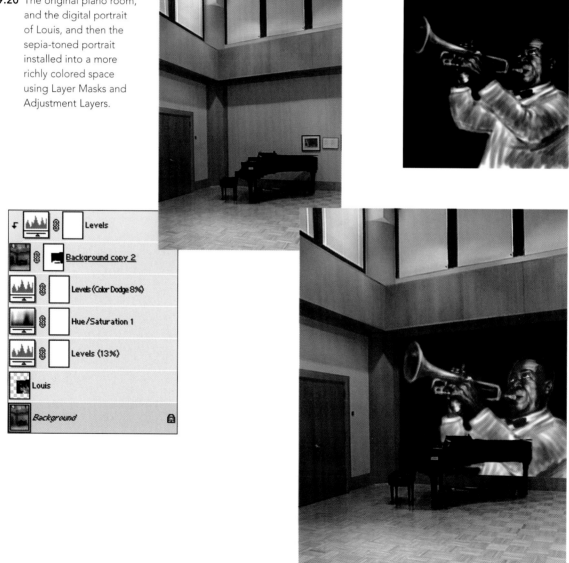

For a variation on the gymnasium theme, I used a different snapshot of the staircase to the same gym used in a project above. For this version I wanted to create a thematic mural of sports balls. In Chapter 3, I describe how I improvised with Blending modes and layers to create the image and how I continued to improvise after the mural was in place. Instead of attaching the Layer Mask to a copy of the Background image, I attached it to the Balls layer so that the balls only were visible between the rails and on the wall. The top layers contain the objects that form the shadows in the corners. The copy of the Background set to Color Dodge Blending mode brightened the whole image (Figure 9.21).

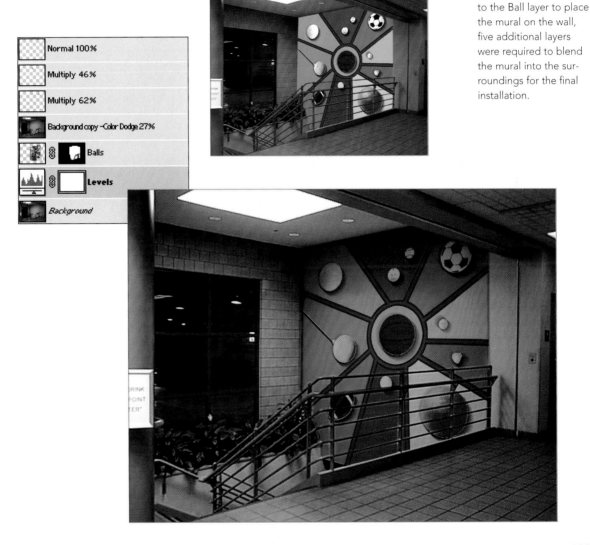

**9.21** Attaching a Layer Mask to the Ball layer to place the mural on the wall, five additional layers were required to blend the mural into the surroundings for the final installation.

**NOTE**

Hold the Command key for Mac or Ctrl for Windows to grab and move a guide. Hide and show guides from the View> Show menu.

To show my client how an image that I created for a possible folding screen would look in her living room, I used another variation of the techniques above. Due to time constraints, I worked very quickly in low resolution (so don't look too closely!). Chapter 3 shows how I made the image. To create the folded appearance of the screen I showed Rulers (Command+R or Ctrl+R) and pulled out guides from the ruler to represent the four panels of the screen. Using the Marquee selection tool, I selected the first panel of the screen. To be able to recall this selection easily, I saved it as an Alpha Channel (by clicking the icon in the Channels palette). I then did the same for each of the other three panels, selecting them and saving the Alpha Channel (Figure 9.22).

**9.22** Creating guides, and saving Alpha Channels for each panel.

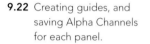

After duplicating the image layer for safekeeping, I loaded the Alpha Channel for the first panel as a selection (Command+click or Ctrl+click on the channel). Then using the Free Transform command (Command+T or Ctrl+T), I distorted the screen to look as if it were folded. To create the accordion-like perspective distortion, I would slide the corner points up and down as needed by holding the Command key (Ctrl for Windows) before I grabbed a corner handle, and then holding the Shift key to constrain the sliding in a vertical direction. After creating the perspective distortion, I used the side handle to slightly compress the panel (viewed at an angle, it would appear slightly narrower). I then repeated this procedure for each of the panels, loading the appropriate Alpha Channel and transforming that panel, making sure that distortion of each panel matched the adjoining one at the point where the panels would be hinged. To make the hinged panels appear more solid, I made a dark-filled copy of the screen shape on a layer below them. To do this I selected all the panels by Command+Shift+clicking on each of the layers (Ctrl+Shift+click for Windows), and then I continued to hold the Shift key and used the Marquee tool to select the gaps between the panels. With the entire outline of the folded screen selected, I saved *it* as an Alpha Channel so that I could easily reselect the entire folded screen (Figure 9.23). Then I created the dark-filled shape behind the screen on a new layer, below the screen panels by filling the selection with a dark Foreground color (Option+Deleting for Mac or Alt+Delete for Windows).

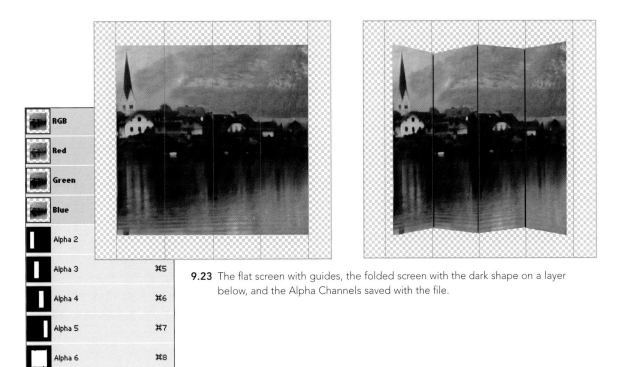

**9.23** The flat screen with guides, the folded screen with the dark shape on a layer below, and the Alpha Channels saved with the file.

To bring my folding screen into my client's living room, I loaded the Alpha Channel that outlined the whole folded screen (Command+click for Mac or Ctrl+click for Windows) and made a flat copy before choosing Edit> Copy Merged. I then pasted the screen into the living room snapshot. I used the Free Transform command to size and position the screen and then created a Layer Mask, so that the screen would fall behind the couch.

To complete the illusion I decided that I needed to change the color cast of the screen to better fit the space, to create some variations in tonality where the screen hinged, to make a drop shadow, and to allow the fern move in front of the screen. I started by placing the screen in a new Layer Set with a the Blending mode set to Normal so I could restrict color and effect changes to only the layers within the set. I then attached a Drop Shadow Layer Style to the screen layer. To restrict the effect of the Drop shadow to the area behind the couch, I attached a Layer Mask to the Layer Set by clicking the Layer Mask icon in the Layers palette. I then used paint and selection tools to create a mask that constrained the effects in the Layer Set to behind the couch. Next, within the Layer Set I created an Adjustment Layer to change the color cast of the screen.

Although I could have done this before, I brought the screen into the living room. I now needed to create shadows for the screen. An active selection limits painting and filling functions to within the selection. So to create the first panel shadow, I created a new layer above the screen and set it to Multiply Blending mode so the darks would darken and not be on top of the screen. I used the Marquee selection tool to create a rectangle that contained the panel top to bottom and matched the panel side to side. With the Gradient tool and the default colors (the D key resets black and white to Foreground and Background), I made a black to white gradient with darks along the edge where the panel should be receding. I repeated this for each of the panels, placing the darks on the receding hinged side, and set the layer to Multiply Blending mode. To constrain the gradient to just the folding screen, in the Layers palette I Command+clicked the Screen layer to load it as a selection (Ctrl+click for Windows), which I then used to create a Layer Mask for the Gradient layer. After it was complete I lessened the effect by reducing the Opacity of the Gradient layer to 57%. Lastly, to allow the fern to show in front of the screen, I painted into the Layer Set Layer Mask (Figure 9.24).

## Installing Three-Dimensional Images

Three-dimensional installations present their own set of problems. Whereas in two-dimensional installations you can distort the images to fit within a space, with three-dimensional work you need to make sure that the viewing angle of your pieces will work with your location. When I showed sculptor Jill Sablosky some simulated installations of my work, she asked me to help with a project of hers.

**9.24** The gradients that created the tonality in the screen shown alone in full opacity, the final layers for the screen (shown with the largest thumbnail size in Palette Options for the Layers palette), and the final installation.

Jill and landscape architecture firm, Glen Gate Company, wanted to find opportunities to collaborate, but they needed samples of how her work would fit into their landscape designs to show prospective clients. Because Jill makes large-scale marble and slate sculptures, the only logical way to do this was through a simulated installation. Glen Gate provided me with a CD filled with high resolution digitized photographs of their landscape designs, and Jill arrived in my studio with photos and scans of her work. Jill and I took some time just looking at the landscape locations and photos of her work trying to find potential compatible pairings. We were looking for similar photographic viewing angles as well as for pieces that would compliment specific locales.

197

In looking through the pairings of sculptures with locales, one immediately looked right. Jill's sculpture "Runic Bridge" (which is actually installed in Texas) would be virtually reinstalled on the property of a Glen Gate client. To begin I created a very rough Layer Mask for the structure. (Until I knew that this would actually work, there was no need to spend the time to make a perfect mask.) I then dragged the Layer to the file containing the new location, which brought the sculpture and its mask to the new file. Once in the new location, I used the Transform tool to scale the piece to fit the space. We used the Move tool to shift its location a few times, and then I cleaned up the Layer Mask. To finish the piece, I fixed the lawn to create a shadow from the sculpture. I used the Clone Stamp tool in layers between the sculpture and the background to relocate areas of shadow to fit the sculpture, and created Levels Adjustment Layers with Layer Masks to darken other areas (Figure 9.25).

**9.25** The sculpture by Jill Sablosky, and the Glen Gate Company's landscape location separate, then combined, scaled, and final.

Other pairings of sculpture with space didn't come together quite as naturally. Before we settled on the second pairing of sculpture and landscape, we tried a number of different pieces in a number of different settings. Finally, we returned to something that didn't quite work and found ways to make it better. For Jill's fountain to fit into the landscape, I had to use Layer Masks to not only isolate the sculpture from its original background, but to reduce the visible portion of the base. To nestle the fountain within the landscape, I used the Clone Stamp tool to patch landscaping into layers above and below the fountain settings (Figure 9.26 and 9.27). (See Chapter 2 for details on how I patch things together.)

**9.26** Trying different sculptures in different places before returning to something that didn't work, and then making it work.

**9.27** Jill Sablosky's fountain reinstalled beside a pond landscaped by the Glen Gate Company.

Now that Jill has seen what we can do, she intends to use this method for her public works and client proposals as well. Instead of simply providing agencies or clients with models, she can provide them with simulated photos of her artwork installed into a specific site. She can now photograph her sculptural models from angles suitable for us to composite into photos of the proposed sites so that viewers can better envision the sculptures in context.

## More Exploration Suggestions

Photograph a gallery or exhibition space and use Photoshop's Compositing and Transformation tools to install your work into the space.

Experiment with changing the scale of your work by simulating installations in different locations or scaled within the same location.

Challenge yourself to create shadows, lights, and patching techniques to better blend your work into its new surroundings.

Improvise with ways to alter your work in the installed space, such as changing the colors using Adjustment Layers, stretching the proportions, or masking out significant portions of it.

Try using Layer Styles such as Bevels and Emboss to create frames for your images.

APPENDIX

# Arranging Your Workspace

To be truly productive in Photoshop, you'll need to take the time to arrange your digital workspace so that it supports your creative workflow. As your relationship with Photoshop evolves, you'll want to refine and improve the setup of your digital workspace so you can increasingly work more efficiently and intuitively. Whenever you find yourself repeatedly working in a way that's frustrating, take the time to figure out a different way to do it. Look in the User Guide, use the online Help, or ask a friend—usually there's some way to fix a productivity problem. Customizing simple settings, such as Auto Layer Select, Resize Windows to Fit, Preserve Transparency, or where you place your palettes can significantly speed up your workflow and reduce your frustration levels. If you repeat a task often, learn how to make an Action to automate the task, and then you can assign it a shortcut key.

In this section I'll share with you some of the details that are essential to arranging *my* digital workspace, but you'll want to make your own adjustments and changes based on your work habits and needs.

## General Computer Setup

The computer can become a big black hole into which you can throw every cent you earn. It's also true that computer stuff will generally get less expensive if you don't immediately purchase the latest hardware—so only get what you need at that moment.

The two areas where your money is always well spent are memory and storage. Purchase as much memory (RAM) for your computer as you can afford. You'll also need a large, fast hard drive, both for storing files and for Photoshop use as a scratch disk to work with large files. Ideally, you'll have a separate hard drive or multiple hard drives for your scratch disk. You'll want enough storage so that you're never faced with "what do I save?" decisions based on drive space.

Whatever equipment you're working with, try to include a large dose of fun in your setup. A good, clear, flat monitor will give you more accurate visual feedback than an economy model, be better for your eyes, and is just plain fun to work with. I currently use two monitors: a larger one for my images and an inexpensive small one on which I place all my palettes. If you don't have the luxury of a giant monitor or two monitors, be aware that the Tab key will toggle your palettes between being visible and hidden (Shift+Tab will keep your Toolbox open). I always use a neutral gray desktop color so that it minimally interferes with the artwork that I'm working on.

Learn how to calibrate your monitor so you can visualize more accurately how your image will look when it's printed. There are commercial software and hardware calibration systems available, so if you require exacting color precision, look into the professional calibration solutions currently available. For my needs, the Adobe Gamma program (that ships with *some* versions of Photoshop) works just fine. I save different gamma settings for each type of output. For instance, when printing to my Epson printer with six-color archival inks, I use a different gamma setting than I use to prepare an image for an RGB film recorder or to a four-color printing press.

## Graphics Tablets

I'm a strong proponent of using a graphics tablet when you're working in Photoshop. When drawing with a tablet, you use a pen-like object called a stylus. To draw a mark or click using the stylus you, press on the tablet with the stylus as you draw to depress the tip of the stylus against the tablet. Because you hold a stylus like a pen, you'll have more control over your marks using the stylus than you can ever achieve using a mouse. Tablets are available in a wide variety of sizes and prices, and most tablets these days are pressure-sensitive. Pressure-sensitive tablets allow you to work with the brushes in Photoshop in ways not possible if you're simply using a mouse.

You can set up your brushes so that they respond to your pressure in a range of variables that include size, color, and opacity. The harder you press with your stylus, the darker, thicker, or more opaque your mark will become. Marks can start out small and transparent and end large and opaque or can be set up to vary in just one of the parameters. For most of my needs, I tend to set up my painting and Eraser tools to be pressure-sensitive in only opacity. I can build up marks gradually and subtlety with gesture and nuance. I use a 6×8 inch Wacom Intuos pressure-sensitive tablet. I like the tablet to be small enough so I can sit back in my chair and have the tablet in my lap. If you're a drafting table kind of artist, then you might prefer a larger, perhaps a 12×12 inch or larger model. If you've never used a tablet, you'll probably find that there is a little bit of a learning curve to the hand-eye coordination. Unless you use the kind of tablet that has a built-in LCD screen, you are looking up at the monitor while drawing on the tablet. The key to aligning your eye and hand is to keep your body square to the tablet. As long as the tablet is lined up with your body, your body can rotate in relation to the screen, and you'll still be able to draw comfortably. Although I have slightly less control drawing with the stylus and tablet than I do with a pencil and paper, being able to easily Undo compensates for any subtle loss of control.

The Wacom styluses, like pencils, generally have erasers on the top end. When you turn your stylus around and press down on the eraser end, Photoshop automatically switches to the Eraser tool. Right-end the stylus again and you're back to your last-used tool. In Photoshop, so you can easily pick up color from your current image—most drawing tools can be transformed temporarily into the Eyedropper tool by holding down Option (for Mac) or Alt (for Windows). You can switch to the Eyedropper tool even more easily if you set up your stylus so that the side button invokes the Option(Alt) key. As you draw, if you then want to pick up a color from your image, hold in the side stylus button to invoke the Eyedropper, click your image to pick up the color, release the side button, and continue to draw with your regular tool.

Some tablets come equipped with a strip of buttons for assigning shortcuts, such as Undo or Copy. I don't tend to use these buttons, as they require me to look down, away from the monitor. I hold my stylus with my right hand, and I keep my left hand on the keyboard (my thumb on the Command key and my index finger ready to Undo) so I can access Undo without looking down at all. If, however, you are left-handed or disabled, Command+Z (Ctrl+Z) is nearly impossible (not to mention adding modifier keys or trying Command+Y); if the keyboard stretches are more of a challenge than a shortcut, the tablet can be a lifesaver. If you do have limited mobility, look for a tablet that comes with a multi-button mouse in addition to the stylus. For a number of years I taught art to a young man with Muscular Dystrophy using the computer. Though Jimmy had a lot of talent, he had very limited mobility and not enough strength to hold the stylus. By using the multi-button mouse and the Wacom tablet, he was able to create wonderful paintings in Photoshop and Painter.

## Saving and Naming Conventions

Computers and hard drives crash, and when they crash they can take all of the work you've created on it to the grave. Earthquakes, hurricanes, and theft also can seriously derail your creative life if you don't take some precautions. The best (and only) way to minimize the chance of your losing work is to save often in incremental versions and back up regularly (if not daily!). Saving incrementally has rescued many hours of my time. When I've found that the current version of a file that I was working with was damaged or corrupted, I could return the last saved state that was still okay. At least I could then rebuild the file from that last safe point instead of having to start all over. For years I used a DAT tape backup system with a great program called Dantz's Retrospect, and now I use a combination of an extra hard drive that I daily drag files to for backup—and I burn CDs. Other perfectly acceptable options are DVD writers, Zip drives, and other removable storage devices. Most people advise that you save copies of important works in a separate location, such as at a family member's house or a safety deposit box. Remember that one of the real beauties of the computer is that you can save things in perpetuity. This ability to archive, however, is only as good as your back-up procedures. If you do not back up your digital work, it isn't protected any better than work in any natural media.

Develop a naming convention that's meaningful to you so that two years from now you can easily find the image you're looking for. Try to keep the names of files so that a series of images will list together alphabetically. For instance, if a whole series is called "The Artist" then the beginning of the naming of all of those images will be "The Artist." Following that you will probably want to give a version number such as "The Artist 1," "The Artist 2," and so on. If you're saving many different versions of an image, you're going to run out of numbers pretty quickly. If you anticipate many versions, you can adopt a convention that the computer world uses. The first version is 1.0, followed by 1.1, 1.2, 1.3, and so on. If you are making somewhat of a leap in artistic, creative, or technical information, then skip right to 1.5. When you make a significant change or move in a different direction, go to the next round numerical level: from 1.3 to 2.0, or 3.1 to 4.0. In addition, I feel it is really important to include some information about the version of the file. For instance: "The Artist 1.1 Green" or "The Artist 1.1 Layered" or "The Artist 1.1 300ppi." Finally, I let Photoshop add the file type extension: PSD, TIF, or JPG. Remember to use PSD to save the maximum amount of information about your file, TIF for saving flat versions to be placed into other applications, and JPG and GIF for smaller file sizes and for use on the web.

NOTE

In earlier versions of Photoshop, saving in TIFF format automatically created files without layers or Alpha Channels; in newer versions you might have to manually choose to exclude layers/channels to create a flattened TIFF file.

## Undos, the History Palette, and Keeping a Log

I've mentioned previously that Undo is probably one of the great inventions of the 20th century. Well, Photoshop takes Undo to the next level. Depending on how much memory you have available, you can have nearly unlimited levels of Undo in Photoshop. If you don't like what you did, Undo. Then continue to Undo again and again until you get back to where you want to be. By default, Undo and Redo toggle with Command+Z (for Mac) and Ctrl+Z (for Windows). To access additional levels of Undo, you must press Command+Option+Z(Ctrl+Alt+Z). Personally, I want to be able to continue to Undo with Command+Z (Ctrl+Z for Windows) until I get to the right spot. To do this, you have to change the keystroke that Photoshop assigns for Redo. In General Preferences, I set my Redo key to Command+Shift+Z because I can do this without looking at the keyboard. The other option for reassigning Redo is Command+Y(Ctrl+Y), but I can't access the Command+Y(Ctrl+Y) easily with one hand. Again, if you are left-handed or have limited mobility, consider looking into a graphics tablet with shortcut buttons or an application called CE Software's QuicKeys, which allows you to assign custom keystrokes to anything.

In addition to multiple levels of Undo, another really wonderful way to rescue what you've been working on within a work session is the History palette. Neither Undos nor the History palette are saved with your file, so they only work within a work session. History stages rely on memory, so the more memory you have available, the more stages you'll be able to rely on. Set the default number of History stages in General Preferences. I tend to use History palette to quickly return to the original state or to return to a state *before* I saved. That's right, if you've accidentally saved your current version, replacing a previous version you wanted to save separately, don't despair. Use the History palette to click the state prior to your current destruction or at the top to the version you first opened. Save the previous version again, return to the latest version, and use Save As to save with a new name. You also can save any current state as a Snapshot in the top of your History palette for easy recall, but don't rely on this in lieu of actually saving something you like!

In addition to saving work in incremental stages, to reconstruct exactly how you achieved a certain effect or result a year from now, it's helpful to keep a journal or log. You can use a word processor, but I prefer to keep a notebook nearby where I note names of files and things that I deem important about the files as I work. I must confess that I just started keeping one a year or so ago and also that my log is a mess. It's my mess, however, and I can find what I need in it when I need to. Hopefully you're one of those neat artists who keep journals that others can follow, but at the very least keep notes that you can follow.

## Ending with the Prints

Because the final form for most of my images is a print, I've always thought of computer art as a printmaking medium. And now, at last, we've entered an era where archival printing is available and almost affordable. For quick proofing you might be able to get away with cheaper options, but always use the best materials for exhibition and sale. I print on 100% rag or cotton papers and with archival inks whenever I can. I print some of my images on my Epson 2000P archival printer, and for others I send my files to a service bureau for printing on a large-format Iris printer (**irisprints.com**). Computer to print technology is forever changing, so do your research. Find out what's best at the time you're ready to order a print from a service bureau or purchase your own printer.

## For More Help with Photoshop

After you've read the manuals that ship with Photoshop and have tried all of the demos that they provide you with, you'll probably still want more help. The following is a list of books that focus on the technical details of Photoshop and/or computer imaging in general. Many of these titles include a version number inserted after the word "Photoshop"— get the latest edition of the book or find the version number that correlates to the version of Photoshop that you're using. But remember, these are books designed to provide you with technical details, so don't get so bogged down that you forget to be creative—remember to experiment and explore!

- ■ *Bert Monroy: Photorealistic Techniques with Photoshop & Illustrator*
  Bert Monroy
  ISBN: 0735709696
  New Riders, Indianapolis, Indiana, **www.newriders.com**

  A beautiful book by a master in Photoshop that focuses on techniques to create photorealistic images.

- ***The Non-Designer's Scan and Print Book***
  Sandee Cohen and Robin Williams
  ISBN: 0201353946
  Peachpit Press, Berkeley, California, **www.peachpit.com**

  This book is a good, basic guide on the technical details of resolution and other basic concepts of working in programs such as Photoshop.

- ***The Painter Wow! Book***
  Cher Threinen-Pendarvis
  Peachpit Press, Berkeley, California, **www.peachpit.com**

  No, this isn't a book on Photoshop, but it is filled with projects that might inspire you to try something new or challenging—maybe even try a new program such as Painter!

- ***Photoshop Artistry***
  Barry Haynes and Wendy Crumpler
  New Riders, Indianapolis, Indiana, **www.newriders.com**

  An intermediate to expert level book dense with technical information about how to achieve things in Photoshop. My editor thinks this is the "best book for serious photographers!"

- ***Photoshop Masking and Compositing***
  Katrin Eismann
  ISBN: 0735712794
  New Riders, Indianapolis, Indiana, **www.newriders.com**

  Finally an in-depth book created to explain how to composite images together and construct perfect masks—and not just any book, but a book by one of the real masters of Photoshop!

- ***Photoshop Power Shortcuts***
  Michael Ninness
  Que, Indianapolis, Indiana, **www.quepublishing.com**

  Every Photoshop shortcut is in here somewhere, and if you want to streamline your workflow, learning shortcuts for things you do often is essential.

- *Photoshop Restoration & Retouching*
  Katrin Eismann
  ISBN: 0789723182
  New Riders, Indianapolis, Indiana, **www.newriders.com**

  Katrin Eismann is one of the best teachers of Photoshop, and this is the book she created to teach you her tricks about retouching and restoring photographs using Photoshop.

- *Photoshop Shop Manual*
  Donnie O'Quinn
  New Riders, Indianapolis, Indiana, **www.newriders.com**

  A deep, technical book that emulates books that walk you through changing the transmission of your car. If you are looking for a book that explains the Smoothness option in the Sketch: Plaster filter, this is the book for you!

- *Photoshop Studio with Bert Monroy*
  Bert Monroy
  ISBN: 0735712468
  New Riders, Indianapolis, Indiana, **www.newriders.com**

  This is the latest book by a talented artist who can make Photoshop do just about anything. He wrote the first book ever written on Photoshop. Since then, Bert has continued to create books that are both beautiful to look at and packed with useful information.

- *The Photoshop Wow! Book*
  Linnea Dayton and Jack Davis
  Peachpit Press, Berkeley, California, **www.peachpit.com**

  This recipe book is packed with tips and techniques for achieving a wide range of effects and results.

- ***Professional Photoshop: The Classic Guide to Color Correction***
  Dan Margulis
  John Wiley & Sons, New York, New York, **www.wiley.com**

  A book that focuses on color correction for professionals who make their living color-correcting or for those who want to know what the professionals know.

- ***Real World Adobe Photoshop***
  David Blatner and Bruce Fraser
  Peachpit Press, Berkeley, California, **www.peachpit.com**

  This book contains in-depth, practical information, with entire chapters devoted to topics such as Color Settings, Selections, or Sharpening.

- ***Real World Scanning and Halftones***
  David Blatner, Glenn Fleishman, and Steve Roth
  Peachpit Press, Berkeley, California, **www.peachpit.com**

  This comprehensive book is devoted exclusively to the details about how you can create the best possible scans for a wide variety of needs.

- ***zenofthepen.org***
  Sharon Steuer and Pattie Belle Hastings
  **www.zenofthepen.org**

  Pattie Belle Hastings and I created this animated tutorial for folks who are ready to take the time to truly master the Pen tool. In addition to the Pen in Photoshop, this course includes lessons for the Pen in Illustrator, FreeHand, InDesign, and Fireworks 4+.

# Techniques at a Glance

The chapters in this book were organized by grouping together similar kinds of creative explorations. Projects progress in complexity both within a chapter, and from early to later chapters. "Techniques at a Glance" was created to help artists and instructors identify the projects that *first* introduce specific techniques, tools, functions, or concepts.

Wrapping your creative exploration around having to learn something specific is one of the oldest tricks of the trade. I often explore new features or tools as the starting point for my projects.

So, if you need to become familiar with a specific tool or function, or if you're an instructor who needs to cover specific technical aspects of Photoshop in a lesson plan, then scan this section to see which projects and chapters best meet your needs. In many cases continuing along in a chapter will provide additional opportunities to explore a technique just introduced.

## Chapter 1: Compositing and the Creative Process

Knowing that you can composite images can change almost everything about the way you work. Projects in this chapter focus on how compositing images at different stages can alter and enhance your creative process.

- Dealing with resolution issues
- Using the Move tool and the Layers palette to combine images
- Working with layers
- Renaming layers
- Scaling with the Free Transform command
- Using keyboard zooming
- Noting percentages in the Options bar
- Nudging with Cursor keys
- Scaling issues and tips

- Changing Blending modes and Layer Opacity
- Creating Layer Masks
- Targeting the layer and Layer Mask icons
- Working with Layer Masks
- Using the Eyedropper tool
- Setting Default colors and Swapping colors
- Filling with Background color
- Using the Gradient tool
- Moving items within layers and reordering layers

- Saving flat versions of a layered file
- Increasing the canvas size
- Using Copy and Paste, and the Move tool to combine images
- Making a Layer Mask from a selection
- Feathering selections
- Viewing masks as an overlay
- Seaming together layers with Layer Masks
- Toggling the Layer Mask on and off
- Linking and unlinking layers and Layer Masks

## Chapter 2: Creative Problem Solving Using Layers

We change our minds, and projects often change direction; but nothing challenges you more to think creatively than having to fix what goes wrong. This chapter uses layers, Adjustment Layers, and Layer Masks to resolve a range of common clean-up issues using different techniques to correct, patch, and replace problems.

- Making flat or "merged" copies of multiple layers
- Rotating and scaling with the Free Transform command
- Setting a layer to Multiply Blending mode to touch-up darks
- Touching up lights with a layer set to Normal or Screen Blending mode
- Equalizing values with Adjustment Layers
- Using Layer Masks for Adjustment Layers

- Inverting selections
- Adjusting layer Opacity to reduce the effect of an Adjustment Layer
- Grouping Adjustment Layers with specific layers
- Duplicating and moving Adjustment Layers
- Grouping and ungrouping layers and Adjustment Layers
- Viewing the Layer Mask alone for mask cleanup

- Using Copy Merged with the Free Transform command to patch gaps in an image
- Using the Clone Stamp tool on a layer above to cover up or patch problems
- Aligned versus not-aligned Clone Stamp tool
- Drawing lines with painting tools
- Using Caps Lock for a precision cursor

## Chapter 3: Improvising with Color Using Layers

This chapter will show examples of creating color "final work" from spontaneous sketches, as well as photographic examples of transforming snapshots into painterly color.

- Changing Color mode from Grayscale to RGB or CMYK
- Naming a layer as you create it
- Setting a layer to Multiply Blending mode to add color while preserving blacks and texture
- Setting a Layer Set to Screen Blending mode to paint in highlights
- Setting a new layer above to Normal Blending mode to touch up with opaque color
- Experimenting with layer Blending modes
- Using Color Burn to place colors into dark portions of an image
- Duplicating layers and reordering them
- Attaching Layer Masks to lesson the effects of layers with Blending modes

- Experimenting with the a layer's Opacity
- Experimenting more with duplicating layers and reordering layers
- Experimenting with Soft Light and Hard Light Blending modes
- Experimenting with Color Dodge and changing the layer Opacity
- Duplicating the Background layer, moving the duplicate, changing the Blending mode, and adding a Layer Mask
- Touching up with a layer above others using painting and Clone Stamp tools
- Saving a flattened TIFF version
- Applying the Rough Pastels filter on a flat image
- Combining different versions of the same image using the Move tool and Layer Masks

- Intensifying an image by duplicating layers and adjusting Blending modes and Opacity
- Applying various filters, such as Blur and Bas Relief, and duplicating layers to create "painterly effects"
- Duplicating original and filtered layers, experimenting with moving the layers, and setting different Blending modes and Opacities
- Adjusting the Opacity and Blending of multiple layers
- Creating Layer Sets
- Merging Layer Sets
- Creating a stylized effect by duplicating layers and adjusting Blending modes to Hard Light and Soft Light

## Chapter 4: Radical Ways to Generate New Ideas from Older, or "Finished" Work

This chapter offers alternatives to starting from blank screens, scans, or photos—ranging from complete distortion with filters to flipping, rotating, stretching, and changing the canvas size, and applying Lighting and Curves.

- Working in RGB Color mode for access to the maximum number of filters
- Using Render and Texture filters to introduce visuals into a blank image
- Working in "progressively stacked layers"
- Duplicating the current version and working on the duplicate
- Experimenting with filters such as Angled Strokes and Wave

- Rotating and flipping layers
- Distorting with Shear
- Transforming selections
- Experimenting with the Curves Adjustment Layer
- Applying Lighting Effects with a Texture Channel
- Trying the Add Noise and Grain filters

- Experimenting with the High Pass filter
- Experimenting with radical changes to Levels and Curves Adjustment Layers
- Experimenting with the Gradient Map Adjustment Layer
- Enlarging your canvas and using the Move tool to combine multiple images in the same file

213

## Chapter 5: Nonlinear Creativity

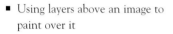

This pivotal chapter focuses on pushing beyond traditional limitations by developing new directions from an earlier phase of an image, and combining multiple states of the same image.

- Using layers above an image to paint over it
- Using the Levels Adjustment Layer to change the color cast of an image
- Using filters such as Brush Strokes and Twirl on a duplicate of your image
- Cropping your image using an active selection
- Using Invert Adjustment Layers
- Rotating your image
- Using layers and Adjustment Layers above an image to alter it
- Using rulers and guides to align images
- Combining similar images in the same file using the Move tool
- Using the Layers palette to hide and show various versions

- Experimenting with Blending modes and Opacity to alter how the different versions interact
- Duplicating layers, moving them around, and changing the Blending modes and Opacities for the duplicates
- Saving incremental flattened versions and reintroducing those versions into the layered file
- Continuing to hide and show layers, reorder layers, and experiment with changing Blending modes and Opacities
- Creating a painterly effect by duplicating an image and combining filtered versions with the original
- Continuing to duplicate layers and adjust the Blending modes, and incorporating the settings of the layer into the layer name

- Using Layer Masks to limit the effect of a duplicated layer with a Blending Mode set
- Creating merged copies of the image at any stage, pasting it back into the layered file, and adjusting its Blending mode and Opacity
- Using Adjustment Layers to change the color or value of the image
- Attaching Layer Masks to Adjustment Layers to limit color or value changes
- After recording the Blending and Opacity changes for each layer, pasting in a different base image and reapplying the effect to the new image, and using Merge Down to apply an effect to the new image
- Creating a new, opaque (black) Layer Mask

## Chapter 6: Compositional Brainstorming

This chapter focuses on working through compositional decisions from overcoming stumbling blocks in traditional media, to creating imaginary places by assembling separate images.

- Using painting tools to work into layers above an image to develop a new creative direction
- Using the Lighting Effects filter to establish a new color and light environment for an image
- Duplicating Lighting Effects layers and adjusting Blending modes and Opacity

- Using Adjustment Layers with Layer Masks to selectively block the adjustment from your image
- Creating a new Adjustment Layer, then creating an opaque Layer Mask so you can selectively use painting tools with whites to apply the adjustment only where you paint

- Experimenting with adjusting the separate channels in a Curves or Levels Adjustment Layer
- Creating a new layer and painting into it, then adjusting the Blending mode and Opacity of the layer
- Creating a large, blank, or colored canvas
- Pasting and moving various images into your colored canvas

- Creating Layer Masks as transitions for each of your image layers
- Filling selections with Foreground and Background colors
- Continuing to bring in new images, hiding and showing various layers, modifying Layer Masks, linking and unlinking layers to move them separately or together, and working quickly and imprecisely
- Using Adjustment Layers to modify and unify the color cast of the different elements
- Patching together elements to create something you're missing in your image

- Creating Layer Sets for groupings of images that are moved together frequently
- Linking layers and using the Free Transform command to alter the elements on the linked layers
- Attaching a Layer Mask to a Layer Set to limit how the Layer Set integrates with the other layers
- Enlarging your canvas and stretching a duplicate of your Background image using Free Transform
- Placing a duplicate of your Background image on top of stretched images and using a Layer Mask to blend elements of the original in with the stretched image

- Using the Clone Stamp tool on layers above to patch and cover undesired elements
- Continuing to create layers, and duplicating layers between others, to weave your composition above and below elements
- Creating Layer Sets to organize elements that you want to keep together
- Duplicating Layer Sets when you want to transform them to keep the originals intact
- Making merged copies of elements and applying filters to the copies
- Applying Layer Effects such as Drop Shadow and Color Overlay to a layer

## Chapter 7: Creating Monotypes from Digital Images

This chapter discusses making monotypes from computer printouts and covers how to prepare the digital image for use as a template, as well as detailing the actual printing process. Both drawn and photographic sources are used as examples for templates for the monotypes.

- Using the Crop tool
- Changing Image Size without altering the resolution of the image

- Using an Adjustment Layer with no adjustment to apply a Blending mode

- Retouching an image with layers above using patching techniques and the Clone Stamp tool
- Flipping the canvas

## Chapter 8: Collaborating with Other Artists or Photographers

Collaborating with others allows you to explore completely different areas artistically than you might encounter on your own. This chapter offers suggestions for how to set up a collaborative relationship and details different approaches for collaborating.

- Filling your canvas or a selection with Background and Foreground colors

- Setting a layer to Overlay Blending mode
- Setting a color for an increased canvas size

- Applying a Hue/Saturation Adjustment Layer

## Chapter 9: Simulating Installations of Your Work

This chapter details a number of different kinds of work in a variety of simulated installations. Preparing work for a simulated installation can involve scaling issues, perspective and lighting changes, and retouching and artistic modifications so that the work fits into its new space.

- Adding to and/or deleting from selections
- Creating layers between an element and its background to create shadows
- Drawing straight lines with the Clone Stamp and Eraser tools
- Distorting in perspective with the Free Transform command
- Selecting active pixels in a layer
- Feathering to round corners of a selection
- Modifying a selection with Enlarge Selection
- Deleting from a selection using active pixels in a layer
- Using Layer Styles to create elaborate frames with Bevel & Emboss and Drop Shadow
- Editing a Layer Styles effect
- Copying an Effects layer to another layer
- Hiding and showing Effects within a Layer Style
- Making a merged copy of selective layers
- Creating an Adjustment Layer within a Layer Set
- Choosing Transparent for new file backgrounds
- Marquee selecting images on a transparent background and then using the Move tool to move them

- Aligning images on multiple layers with guides
- Using the Crop tool to resize and rotate while cropping
- Entering transformations with the Options bar
- Scaling an image with Resampling on
- Using the Pen tool
- Saving a Pen path
- Making a selection from a path
- Saving a selection as an Alpha Channel
- Making a selection from an Alpha Channel
- Using the Auto Select Layer feature
- Loading an Alpha Channel to select an area for copying
- Reloading an Alpha Channel or a path in preparation to receive something being pasted
- Creating a Clipping Layer
- Modifying a selection by creating a Border
- Using the Edit> Stroke and Edit> Fill commands
- Using Gradient Layer Masks to gradually blend the effect of a layer to layers below
- Using the Screen and Soft Light Blending modes, and Opacity to simulate the application of an image to fabric

- Adding a Layer Mask to a duplicate of a Background layer so part of it can appear on top of the rest
- Using the Pen tool to work on a Layer Mask
- Inverting a mask
- Applying the texture of an original by overlaying a duplicate and changing Blending modes
- Attaching a Layer Mask to an image to place it within a space
- Using rulers and guides to aid in selections
- Moving, hiding, and showing guides
- Loading an Alpha Channel to select and Free Transform a portion of a layer
- Using Free Transform to compress a selection
- Adding Alpha Channels to a selection
- Using a Layer Mask to restrict the effect of a Layer Set containing the Drop Shadow Layer Style
- Dragging a layer with a Layer Mask into another file
- Working with rough Layer Masks until scaling and positioning is determined, then just cleaning up masks for final versions

# Index

## G

## H

## I-J-K

## U

## V

## W-X-Y-Z

PHOTOSHOP® 7

**Photoshop 7 Killer Tips**
Scott Kelby, Felix Nelson
0735713006
$39.99

**Photoshop 7
Down & Dirty Tricks**
Scott Kelby
0735712379
$39.99

**Photoshop 7 Magic**
Sherry London,
Rhoda Grossman
0735712646
$45.00

**Photoshop 7 Artistry**
Barry Haynes,
Wendy Crumpler
0735712409
$55.00

**Inside Photoshop 7**
Gary Bouton, Andy Anderson,
Robert Stanley, J. Scott Hamlin,
Daniel Will-Harris,
Mara Nathanson
0735712417
$45.00

**Photoshop Studio with
Bert Monroy**
Bert Monroy
0735712468
$50.00

**Photoshop Restoration
& Retouching**
Katrin Eismann
0789723182
$49.99

**Photoshop Type Effects
Visual Encyclopedia**
Roger Pring
0735711909
$45.00

**Creative Thinking in
Photoshop**
Sharon Steuer
0735711224
$45.00

New Riders

VOICES THAT MATTER™

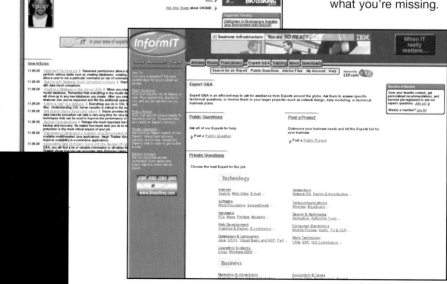